THE GREAT NORTH RUN
THE FIRST 25 YEARS
and my part in it

2-99

THE GREAT NORTH RUN
THE FIRST 25 YEARS
and my part in it

THE GREAT NORTH RUN
THE FIRST 25 YEARS
and my part in it

opposite: John Giles/PA/Empics
Roger Coulam

KENSINGTON WEST PRODUCTIONS

Owen Humphreys/PA/Empics

Kensington West Productions Ltd

5 Cattle Market, Hexham

Northumberland NE46 1NJ

ISBN 1 902990218

Author:	Richard Lewis
Editors:	Mike Kearney, Peter Killick, Tanya Marshall, Barry Roxburgh, Helen Spearman
Researcher:	Mike Kearney
Race Results:	David Martin
Production:	Joanna Walton
Front Cover Design:	David Wardle
Designed by:	Diane Ridley
Origination by:	Prepress Ltd
Printed in:	China

The author would like to thank the following people for their help in the production of this book: Simon Turnbull (Independent on Sunday), Rob Maul (Sunday Times), Hayley Lewis, Melodie Driscoll and Helen Mitchinson.

Photographic contributions from:
John Williamson
John Giles/PA/Empics
Roger Coulam
Owen Humphreys/PA/Empics
Evening Chronicle And Journal Ltd
Mark Shearman
Norman Potter/Central Press/Getty Images
Jim Gibson
Kevin Gibson
Tony Duffy/Getty Images
Nova International
Bryn Lennon/Getty Images
Hulton Archive/Getty Images
Steve Powell/Getty Images
Katy Melling
Fairfax Suburban Newspapers Auckland
Frederic Lewis/Getty Images
Ad Infinitum
Getty Images
South Shields Gazette
Picture Loan: Keith And Katherine Denton
Tanya Marshall
Michael Steele/Getty Images
Picture Loan: Ray Scott
John Caine

1 The thrill of the moment as the run is completed.
2 It is a sight to take your breath away: 48,000 plus runners in their quest for success.
3 The scaffolding taking shape signals the start of a long weekend for the more usually tranquil South Shields coast.
4-5 The start of the Great North Run combines a mixture of excitement and tension but the atmosphere is extraordinary whatever.

INTRODUCTION

We originally planned to record the story of the BUPA Great North Run to celebrate its 21st running but you know how it is, so much to do… and now, some years later, we've published it to coincide with our 25th anniversary year.

In a similar way to the run itself we had a fairly clear objective. To record the story for those who want to know of how it came together – well we might not be around for the 50th running. We also wanted to illustrate the race with some high quality images as well as capture its mood through some personal memories from great runners, some well-known celebrity runners and just a sampling of the many that give the run its heart and soul.

We also thought it significant to record the results of the race and how they came about and to offer brief insights into what was happening each year. We wanted to produce something visually exciting – we wanted to catch the mood of the race from the elite runners to someone running 'for my mum'. We wanted to show the iconic pictures of the Tyne Bridge as well as less well-known views.

One thing I realised from an early stage though, is that this is not my story nor is it that of Nova International. No, it is a story that embraces over 650,000 different episodes. All of which have a differing twist, whether it be the satisfaction of a personal best or just getting home. To commemorate these hugely satisfying tales would take an encyclopaedia, but we realise that to many their reasons for running are very personal, and so we decided to celebrate the part of these 650,000 plus people by including a 'my part in it' where personal memories, recollections and thoughts, as well as times can be recorded for future years. It is, if you like, your story of the Great North Run.

As you can imagine it is impossible to thank everyone who has helped us develop the Great North Run – there have been so many. They all know who they are and we thank them all. There are also many whom we have never met and will never meet, who run perhaps only once – or even year after year. We are pleased to thank them as well, for making the Great North Run the biggest half-marathon in the world, something of which all of those 650,000, as well as their families and supporters, can be deeply proud.

Brendan Foster

I worked with my friend Robin Brown in the Boots Factory in Airdrie. Robin had taken part in the Great North Run since 1985, and in 1996 he asked me if I would like to, because he had a spare application form. I said 'No' because I had never run the distance before.

Around Christmas time of 1996, he came to me with a filled in application form for the 1997 run which only required my signature. I tried to make my excuses but he wouldn't take no for an answer. He even covered the cost - telling me it was my Christmas present.

I ran it, and we had the most fantastic time. We repeated it in 1998.

Then, came April 8 1999. Robin and I had finished our run home from work, I said goodbye and that I would see him tomorrow. I had just entered my house when the telephone rang. It was a member of Robin's family to say that he had collapsed and died just after he had got home. He was only 57. The post mortem revealed heart failure and the doctor told his wife, Isobel, that he would have died 10 years earlier if had not kept up his running.

I have run the Great North Run every year since then. I feel Robin is with me every step of the way. As long as I am fit and able, I shall continue to run in the memory of my friend Robin Brown.

Archie McKennan
Retired, Airdrie

1981

The first Great North Run took place against the backdrop of a troubled summer. Across the UK, riots set city centres ablaze from Brixton in London to Toxteth in Liverpool. Yet the brief turmoil of the 'summer of discontent' was forgotten once streets across the kingdom were hung with red, white and blue to celebrate the Royal Wedding. Perhaps it was the wave of romantic patriotism that swept across the country in the wake of Prince Charles' fairytale marriage to Lady Diana Spencer, that helped make Brideshead Revisited the most watched television drama of the year. This nostalgia for Pimms and punting also saw a new breed of Briton emerge into the social spotlight, dubbed the 'Sloane Rangers'. But if you weren't wearing a waxed cotton coat or green wellies, nor sporting the heavy eyeliner favoured by Adam Ant and the New Romantics, chances were you'd be dressed in lycra and legwarmers thanks to the publication of Jane Fonda's Workout Book which launched the decade's craze for aerobics.

2004

Despite the defeat and the capture of Saddam Hussein, criticism of the war in Iraq continued to grow. In Britain, continued concern about the war resulted in two government investigations. The first, the Hutton Report, cleared the government from any blame over the death of Dr David Kelly; Doctor Kelly, a leading weapons expert, had told a BBC journalist that perhaps the government had been less than truthful about its justification for the war. The journalist duly claimed that the government had 'sexed up' intelligence reports concerning Iraq's nuclear and biological weapons. After Hutton, the Butler Report also exonerated the government from any accusations that it had deliberately misled the public over claims that Iraq could launch nuclear or biological weapons within 45 minutes. Once again, it was sport that provided a welcome break from the tortuous world of politics, with British athletes winning a record tally of medals at the Athens Olympics, including two golds for runner Kelly Holmes.

6 The picture that made the headlines as the Great North Run makes its first crossing of Newcastle's Tyne Bridge in 1981.
9 The Tyne Bridge remains the iconic landmark of the BUPA Great North Run and the city of Newcastle.

JANE TOMLINSON

my part in it...

Diagnosed with breast cancer when she was just 26 years old. Inspirational runner and fund raiser. Jane completed the 2002 Great North Run in 1:51. In January 2005, Jane announced that her fundraising had topped her £1m target.

I'VE got great memories of the Great North Run. In 2002, before my first run, my husband Mike and I trained hard in the build-up to the race. We bluffed and double-bluffed about how well our training was going – both determined to surprise each other on the actual day. My targets were to beat Mike and get under 1:55.

I was really struggling mid-way through the run, but by 11.5 miles I knew I could get there. I came in at 1:51, some time ahead of Mike who claimed that he'd been slowed down by having to give an interview during the run. Just like the London Marathon, you come across so many great stories and people during the race, but somehow it seems to me that there's more of a human 'feel' at the Great North Run.

My abiding memory, though, has to be as I approached the finish. There was fantastic support from thousands of people. It was a wonderful family occasion as Mike and I were greeted by my children, my mother, my mother-in-law and my late father-in law, Jack.

Jack was a runner himself in his youth. He'd been too ill to come to see me at the London Marathon earlier in the year and so it was especially moving for us to see him as we crossed the finishing line at South Shields. Sadly, he's since died but it remains a wonderful memory of a fantastic occasion.

www.janesappeal.

Kevin Gibson

11 At the start of the 1997 run thousands of athletes make their way from Newcastle's Central Motorway to South Shields

Owen Humphreys/PA/Empics

FOREWORD

I am not particularly proud of my crystal ball. Nearly fifty years ago I wrote an article about transport in the year 2000. I forecast a brisk tourist trade to the moon. I forecast that on entry to the motorway you would hand over your car to automatic control and be woken when it was time to branch off. And there was a lot more in similar vein.

It did not seem far-fetched, given the transformation of transport since my father's childhood before the invention of the car and the aeroplane. In fact of course nothing much has changed very dramatically. Planes go a bit faster and, thanks to congestion, cars and buses go a bit slower. But no revolution.

Now if anybody had forecast to me fifty years ago that running long distances would become hugely popular, that hundreds of thousands of people around the world would vie for coveted places in marathons and half-marathons and, weirdest of all, that lots of those people would be women, I should not just have been totally disbelieving. I should have been seriously worried about the forecaster's state of mind.

When I was competing there were no runners to be seen on the roads or in the parks. For three years as a student at Magdalen College Oxford I carried my bag, with towel and running kit inside, over the bridge to the Iffley Road running track half a mile away. Never once did I change in my room and jog to the track. Running about in public just was not done.

Our view of marathon runners was also very different. There were not many of them; all of course were men; and they were regarded as strange and eccentric beings; more like something out of the circus than a part of mainstream athletics. What they did was seen as extraordinary and courageous. Rather like the human cannonball – amazing and intrepid but was it really worth it? And anyway hardly a normal sporting event.

So the running boom, when it came, was a total surprise to me. As was the astonishing growth of the big city marathons. It all amounted to a considerable social revolution. But there is no more exciting story in all of this than the one told in the pages of this book.

It is a story of high athletic achievement with great races and fine records from many of the world's greatest runners. There are also in the pages that follow stories about people of no particular athletic ability whose lives have been changed by their experience of the Great North Run.

The achievement of a physical goal beyond their expectations has opened up for many an entirely new idea about the wider goals they can set themselves in life. Thousands of others have simply found that training for the run has given them an energy and sense of wellbeing that has led them to alter their lifestyle.

I have always hesitated to argue to my children or to anybody else who has had to listen to my advice that regular exercise is a must for everybody. A healthy mind, whatever the Latin tag claims, does not always reside in a healthy body. I have known a good many very healthy minds in much neglected bodies and vice versa.

We are all different. But it does seem to be true that most people function better with regular exercise; and for many, running – however slowly – is best of all. For hundreds of thousands of years our early human ancestors depended for their survival upon an ability to outrun their prey – not so much to sprint faster but to keep running for longer.

So natural selection ensured that the will and ability to keep running was hard-wired into our make up. When today we accustom ourselves to running we are responding to some of our deepest instincts. We know that we are doing something that is for us – for the particular animals we are – just utterly natural.

The Great North Run and the whole running/jogging phenomenon has surely made a huge contribution to human health. It must have saved and prolonged the lives of thousands and added to the happiness and fulfilment of millions.

Twenty-five years on, Brendan Foster has every reason to be proud of his creation. He was one of Britain's greatest distance runners and all the more memorable because, so it seemed to me, his achievements came more from strength of character than natural ability. But he may well be remembered even more as an impresario of distance running.

With his colleague John Caine he has created "Great Runs" up and down Britain, out to Ethiopia and who knows where next. The Great North Run is the biggest half-marathon in the world and perhaps the most remarkable of all the events spawned by the running boom.

I marvel every year at the London Marathon founded by my friends and contemporaries Chris Brasher and John Disley. I have always applauded them for doing more for London's sense of community than anybody since Adolf Hitler! But once every big capital city followed the Americans by organising a marathon, there was, I suppose, always going to be one in London.

Mark Shearman
opposite: Norman Potter/Central Press/Getty Images

An abiding memory: the poignant story of Ray Greaves who watched the first Great North Run with his daughter who was enthralled by the sight of the runners. Unfortunately she died of cancer and Ray founded the North of England Children's Cancer Research charity, based at the R.V.I in Newcastle, in her memory. I was inspired to run for them for many years and am glad to have played my part in the millions raised for charity

If Ian Yarrow, my friend who lives near the end of the run, and I manage to complete this year's GNR this will be the 25th year we have both competed, and the 25th year that Ian has allowed me to go to his house for a shower and refreshments after the run. He says he and his wife don't mind as long as I don't come more than once a year!

Joe Flegg
65, Retired Teacher, Alnwick

12 Sir Christopher Chataway relives the historic moment, 50 years later.
13 Chris Chataway (right) and Chris Brasher did their bit to help Roger Bannister to sporting history as he broke the four minute mile for the first time.
14-15 Superwomen, supermen and a posse of children taking part in Saturday's Junior Great North Run.

13

Without Chris and John it would not have been so good but there was bound to be a London Marathon. In contrast there was nothing inevitable about a world-class half-marathon in Newcastle. That came solely out of the brains and drive of Brendan and his team.

So what is the downside? What are the disadvantages of all this running about?

When I look at veteran athletes – and in the mirror – I sometimes think that, while running makes you feel younger, it also makes you look older. But so what ? There comes a stage anyway when it is not much good worrying about how you look. Today I don't mind running in the streets and parks and, as I do so, the bystander no doubt sees a geriatric shuffle. But to me it feels like an easy rhythmic stride – and after all it is me I am doing it for!

More insidious is obsession. Any enthusiasm can outrun all reason and some runners can have their lives consumed by their sport. A compulsion always to cover scores of miles each week can get in the way of enjoying or achieving anything else. Gordon Pirie was one of the most brilliant runners of my generation and one of the first to realise the benefits of heavy training. But when in later life he would hand you a visiting card with his total mileage to date (it got to about 250,000 I think) you realised that in return for success the sport had exacted a heavy price.

While Gordon kept on running to the exclusion of all else, I made the opposite mistake. The way Roger Bannister and I and many university athletes trained was based on the ideas of the previous generation – men like the Oxford New Zealander Jack Lovelock, winner of the Olympic 1,500 metres in Berlin. We were anxious not to get stale and our training was ridiculously light. So racing against the likes of Emil Zatopek and Vladimir Kuts, who both had far more intense training regimes, was a very painful business.

I loved the achievement and the excitement and revelled in the successes, when they came along, but I could not say that, in any ordinary sense of the word, I enjoyed the major races. They just hurt too much. So when I gave up competing at the age of twenty-five, I then thankfully took practically no exercise – a silly decision and one that I was lucky not to suffer for.

It was not until my early fifties that I started to run regularly again – just ten or twelve miles a week of slow jogging before breakfast and at the weekend. And then in my sixties with more training I began running in cross-country races with my old club Thames Hare and Hounds. I was never last and I discovered the secret of enjoying

races, which had eluded me when young – if it starts to hurt, slow down!

A couple of years ago at the BBC Sports Personality of the Year programme I was sitting with Brendan. As this was to choose the fiftieth winner and I had been the first, I was allowed to bring my two youngest sons Adam and Mat. By the end of the evening we had all agreed – much to our surprise – to start in the Great North Run. I had never run as far as a half-marathon in my life and they had not run in a race of any kind since they were children.

Adam's girl friend Vicky decided to join in and so did another son, Ben – both of them also complete novices. Eight months later there we all were on an early Sunday morning in Newcastle, shivering with trepidation on the start line with only one thought on our minds – why on earth were we there?

And of course... it was wonderful. The bands, the crowds, the sense of occasion, the sheer fun of it all. I was lucky enough to have an experienced road runner, Derek Hull, alongside me with a word of advice when I was going too fast or too slowly and a generally reassuring presence. When I got to ten miles and it was only just over an hour and a quarter and I felt fine, I thought it must be just another of those vainglorious dreams, from which it is such a disappointment to awake.

We all finished and had our stories to tell. Mat, who had just had three years at Newcastle University, was surprised and delighted at one point by the numbers shouting out for him. He had never realised he had acquired such a following. Then he saw that he was overtaking the great Matthew Pinsent.

It was some time after twelve miles that I realised that a disgraceful mistake must have been made in the measurement of the course. What was said to be the last mile must have lasted for at least five. Nonetheless we are all doing it again this year – and this time it did not even need any persuasion from Brendan.

I hope that among the readers of this book will be many of you who had never thought of running; that you will be fascinated by the history of this great event and by the human stories around it; that you will decide gradually to get yourselves in shape and to give it a go. Will you succeed in finishing? How fast will you do it? Certainly don't rely on my crystal ball. But you may well surprise yourself. On the day of the race and in the years thereafter.

Sir Christopher Chataway

THE STORY OF THE GREAT NORTH RUN

Gateshead
Newcastle
A692

Tony Duffy/Getty Images

IT is the morning of September 26th 2004 and we are standing in the middle lane of a motorway in Newcastle. We cannot move. The scene in front of us is extraordinary. It is an ocean of colour, a sight to take your breath away. A traffic jam of 49,000 people.

We cannot see where this vast human line ends. It stretches back a mile, perhaps more, a mass, locked together, in preparation for a challenge. For some it is their job, for others it is their hobby, but for the majority it is their mission; an obsessive desire to prove to themselves that they can achieve their own landmark on one of Britain's finest sporting days. It is the morning of the BUPA Great North Run and the start line is alive with anticipation.

Some people are standing waiting, others are jogging on the spot; some are anxious, many are smiling, others are just motionless. Their questions are probably all the same.

Have the laces been tied? Will I drink enough water? Have I prepared properly? What if I don't make it? What if I do, will I want to come back next year? Can I put myself through this again?

The countdown is almost over. It has been nine months since the process began with a signature on a form that has led to this moment, after weeks of training, pounding the streets to be ready for a day that most will never forget. No time to pull out now. Nowhere to run, except in one direction, the 13.1 miles that lie ahead.

Suddenly, the concentration is broken by the whirr of a helicopter, a noise in the distance that is growing louder. It is overhead and thousands of eyes look upwards as it comes in to land on a bank of grass.

A young man jumps out. He is balding, he is wearing a blue singlet and white shorts, and the muttering from the pack begins. They do not recognise him, but they think he must be someone special because your average runner does not arrive by helicopter. They are wrong. He could not be more ordinary; but he is the epitome of why 49,000 people are waiting for the gun to fire, because this is no ordinary run.

He shakes hands with three officials. One directs him to a position behind the more familiar faces of the elite runners who are waiting at the head of the field. He stops. He looks at his watch. Few will know why he is here, fewer still would be able to keep a dry eye if they knew his reason.

His name is Findlay Young and he has spent a year waiting for 9.50 am on September 26th 2004. The clock ticks on, it reaches the time and despite all the noise, all the excitement, all the emotion and the thousands of people around him, he blocks everything out to just reflect for a moment.

Twelve months earlier, he was sitting in a hospital room waiting to learn if he still had cancer. Just imagine how this feels. His doctor broke the news. He was given the "all clear"; tides of emotion ran through him, but he did what many a runner does, as a matter of course… he looked at his watch: the time was 9.50am.

He wanted to commemorate that exact moment – the wonderful emotion he felt then and how he imagined he would feel a year later. When he flicked through a calendar to this day an idea came to him.

"The Great North Run…" he says, his sentence trailing off, "I'd often watched it on television. Something stirred inside me when I saw it was due to take place on the same date. What better way could I celebrate being alive than by being here as part of something which leaves you bursting with more inspiration than you could possibly imagine?"

The organisers of the Great North Run could never have imagined that the race they had worked tirelessly to develop would affect people so much.

Not just in the way it was mentioned in the pub or before kick-off on a football Saturday, but in the way it has become part of the fabric of their lives. On this morning, it was the vehicle for celebrating being alive for this cancer patient.

Findlay Young could make it, but only with some extra help. On the morning of the Great North Run, Newcastle is at a standstill. There are no roads in, few roads out and for any latecomers, only one option: a private helicopter.

But there's a twist. In the past 24 hours, Young has already run three other half-marathons, part of the extraordinary target he set himself and one which would conclude with the BUPA Great North Run – his reason for running in the first place. It has been some experience, but he did not know what to expect when his journey from his last race in Wales took him high above the start line in Newcastle. He was stunned.

"I looked out of the windows of the helicopter and all I could see was this train of people that was growing longer the closer we got to it. It was the most amazing thing I have ever seen."

Below him were the legions who would take an estimated 11.5 million breaths between them as they ran from Newcastle to the North Sea coast that fronts South Shields. Among them, every postcode in Britain has someone representing it and by the finish, more than £10 million will have been raised for charity.

This is a morning when real life is suspended for a few hours and in its place 49,000 people fulfil their own dreams. Young was celebrating the triumph of being alive and a stubbornness not to give in against all the odds.

16-17 Brendan Foster pounds out the miles in the spring of 1976 when the Great North Run was not even a distant thought.
18 Findlay Young, runner and example to one and all.
19 The crowd at the start begins to swell as Newcastle's Central Motorway is turned to a people jam.

JOHN MOTSON *my part in it...*

Front line commentator with BBC Television for over 25 years with regular contributions to Match of the Day, Grandstand and Sportsnight.

I've done it nine times and only in 2003 did I take more than 2 hours. My best time was in 1997 when I did 1 hr 40 – but it's not just the race it's the whole weekend. It's genuinely the pleasure of being part of the whole event – it's a great social event which may also have affected some of my times.

One year, 2001 I believe it was, I wasn't happy with my preparation and I was a bleeding mess (literally). Anyway, I stopped to do an interview after six miles – and was promised some vaseline after nine – when I was due to do another interview. There was nothing there so I struggled to the first aid tent at the finish – with blood covering me, I wanted something to rub the gunge away.

One of the organisers, John Caine, is a great guy and this memory was typical of him: for one reason or another I'd had bad luck with the special V.I.P. bus they had laid on (one got badly stuck in traffic and another broke down) so I said to Cainey, "I'll do your run but forget the bus." The next year he organised a helicopter for me and Ray Stubbs – that was typical of the man. Nothing was ever too much trouble.

Funnily enough though, it was Brendan who was the main reason for me running – but as a runner not the organiser. He got a lot of us fairly unfit broadcasters keen on having a go.

I love my records and stats and I recently had my times sent through. I still maintain I would have done better in 2003 but I actually fired the starting gun that year with Mark Knopfler and I then ran the first mile too quickly trying to keep up – I went off too quick but I made a lot of friends. One person who John Caine had got to run round with me was Ray Scott – he was my minder. Well we became friends and Ray recently came down and we did my local half-marathon.

I won't be running in 2005 but I'll definitely come up and sample and enjoy as always the many fringe events.

Brendan Foster (left) and Mike McLeod recover after the men's 10,000 metres, Commonwealth Games, Edmonton, 1978. Foster won the Gold Medal.

Chapter 1

RUNNING FOR GOLD

BRENDAN Foster also refused to take 'No' for an answer in creating this extraordinary run. But he never imagined it would be like this. Not even he could have anticipated that it would become the biggest half-marathon in the world.

It was conceived, by chance, in New Zealand, and became a reality in Newcastle. Now his 'baby' is in its 25th year and is a thriving, healthy creature that is growing each year, every 12 months finding fresh friends and arousing new and amazing challenges.

When Foster first heard of Findlay Young's mission, from the depths of despair to the start line of his run, he sat back in his office in Newcastle.

After more than two decades, nothing should surprise him about what the Great North Run brings to bear. But this did. "What can you say to that?" says Foster. "A man is celebrating being alive by wanting to be part of our run. It is beyond words."

It is only one story in a million – the number of people who have been connected with a race that celebrates its silver anniversary in 2005.

But for every theme and every tale and every record-seeking performance, whether it be by someone as professionally brilliant as Paula Radcliffe, or as brave as Findlay Young, it all goes back to one person: Brendan Foster.

One of the most enduring British sporting images of the 1970s is the distance runner with his head down, showing the ultimate effort in every race. Brendan Foster won both affection and respect in the eyes of the public, because when he ran, whether it was over 1,500 metres, 3,000m, 5,000m or 10,000m, he gave his all.

Take 1974. He promised to break a world record at a meeting on his home track in Gateshead and he kept his word. It was the year that defined him as one of Britain's greatest athletes. That summer he won the 5,000m gold medal at the European Championships, a victory combined with his world record that led to him being named as the BBC Sports Personality Of The Year.

In 1976, he was British athletics' only medal winner at the Montreal Olympic Games, in the 10,000m. In 1978, he was the Commonwealth champion at the distance but by 1980, when he

I did the first race in 1981 when I was 44 and although I was a member of Elswick Harriers that was my first half-marathon distance. The crowds and the atmosphere were fantastic, not seen before in local running events, and the personal excitement and satisfaction I experienced sowed the seeds for my love of the event. My wife and I have completed at least 20 Great North Runs together, her last being in 2003.

My best time was 1:18:45 in 1982. Since then I have sustained an ankle joint injury and my time drifted out to 2:20 in 2003. However, with regular training at the gym on the low-impact CV machines, my time improved in 2004 and my target now is to get to the start of my 25th Great North Run. Until 2002 my mother, now 95 years old, always provided my first feeding station in the race at 3.5 miles. I have many happy memories of the run and it will be a very sad day when I have to stop taking part in this event, but long may it continue.

Kevin Lowdon
68, Engineer, Gateshead

23

was heading towards retirement, he was forging an idea to stage a race of his own.

Brendan Foster was born on January 12, 1948. He did not start running until he was in his early teens when he joined Gateshead Harriers, one of five athletics clubs in the area. The club was the most successful at both track and cross-country, and it was only six miles from his Hebburn home. It was accessible and it demanded excellence.

Foster was the eldest of six children, whose father Frank worked for the Council and whose mother Margaret kept the home. At school he enjoyed many subjects and although passionate about sport, running was still very much an amateur pursuit. Those were not the days when you could make a living out of being an athlete, but you could still find a hero or two.

His idol was Peter Snell, the big, muscular New Zealander who had broken the world record for the mile in 1962, having won the Olympic 800m title in Rome in 1960 before achieving the middle distance double, of the 800m and 1,500m titles in Tokyo in 1964. It was something that Foster watched with awe, dreaming of one day being an Olympian himself.

Snell had a major effect on his life. As Foster says: "I distinctly remember the first time I saw him. In 1960, when the Olympics were held in Rome, I was a 12 year old playing football for my local team and I dreamed of being 'the next Jackie Milburn' and playing centre-forward for Newcastle.

"I did not know much about athletics at that time, although my dad was a big sports fan. I remember running home from school in my uniform with my satchel on my back to watch the Olympic Games in Rome. On the television, there was this big, strong New Zealand bloke, who nobody had ever heard of.

"On the first night he won his heat in the 800m, breaking the New Zealand record and then he won the semi-final. In the final, he ran against the world record holder Roger Moens, from Belgium.

"Going into the Games, Snell's best time was over three seconds slower than Moens, the record holder. Coming into the final, I remember thinking: 'My God, I hope he wins this.' With 200m left to go in the race, the TV commentator said: 'And now the world record holder hits the front.' I thought to myself: 'Come on, you can do this.' And then Peter Snell edged past him and won the race. For an unknown New Zealander to win was a big shock. I remember him as the big figure in the black vest with the silver fern on the front of his shirt. I thought to myself: 'That vest is fantastic, I'd love to run in one of those.'

Steve Powell/Getty Images

"By the time the next Olympics arrived in Tokyo, Snell was the world record holder for the 800m. At that time, I was interested in athletics because I had been running at school and in cross-country races. It was 1964. I had read all the books on the New Zealand runners, who used to run through the ferns and over the hills outside Auckland.

"Snell beat the world record for the 800m by one-and-a-half seconds. Nobody has beaten the 800m record by that margin since. He was then holder of the mile record as well. So, going into Tokyo, I wished I had a tall black flag to support him.

"When it came to the 1,500m final, he won that as well. His last lap in the Olympic Games was faster than Steve Ovett, Seb Coe and Steve Cram when they broke the 1,500m world record. The other interesting thing that not many people know is that this was his first 1,500m race ever (at the Tokyo Games). In New Zealand he only ever ran the mile.

"I always say to people that if I had not been a good runner, I would still have enjoyed being a bad runner. If it had not been for Peter Snell, I might have been the next Jackie Milburn, but for one key fact – I wasn't good enough!"

Snell brought the glamour that inspired Foster's enthusiasm for distance running. There was no obvious reason for it, except that perhaps heroes have a way of finding a line of succession.

Since 1885, a baton has been passed from one generation in the North East to another. By the early 1970s, it was seeking a new incumbent and Foster took it on to a new level, even though those before him had achieved the highest recognition in their own day and had paved the way for future runners. One of them had a play written about him, another was decorated as the region's first Olympian. They were the standard bearers for generations to come.

These roots, well over 100 years old, were started by the heroics of an athlete known as The Black Callant.

By the late 1800s, wagers and back-handers were the rule in the amateur world of athletics. They meant runners could unofficially earn some money from their talent. The first to progress from the North East was James Rowan. He would train on the half-marathon route between Morpeth and Newcastle. Before the arrival of the Great North Run, it was the area's most famous run; it lasted for 100 years until the 2004 running became its last.

Rowan was an athlete of glorious ability, but his story had a tragic ending. He was the British Three Mile and 10-Mile champion. He was only 5 ft 6 ins, but on the track he was a runner of breathtaking speed.

He would travel regularly to London, to Hackney Wick in the East End. It was there that spectators would pack into the stadium, paying a shilling a time to watch him run. He was known as The Black Callant from his Caledonian roots: it was the Scottish description of a young boy. But at 28, Rowan contracted tuberculosis and died. He is buried in an unmarked grave at Gateshead Cemetery.

Jack White, dubbed the Gateshead Clipper because of his speed, followed the heroism of Rowan to become one of the British greats of the last century.

His national record of 29 minutes, 44 seconds for six miles lasted 14 years and he ran at Hackney too, famously beating a legendary Native American runner known as Deerfoot.

White ran in America as well, defeating all opposition, before, at the turn of the century, becoming a coach at Cambridge University and then at Chelsea Football Club.

A tradition was growing, one which Jack Potts, a Saltwell Harrier, continued when he won the AAA and National cross-country titles in the early 1930s before Alex Burns became Tyneside's first Olympian in 1932 in Los Angeles. He ran in the 5,000m and 10,000m, and returned four years later to compete in the same events in Berlin. He died at the age of 95 in May 2003 and his life was celebrated in 2004 when a plaque was dedicated to his memory at the Black Bull Public House in Barrack Road in Elswick – where the Harriers used to have their headquarters.

In 1962, Saltwell Harrier's John Anderson ran for Britain in the 5,000m at the European Championships in Belgrade and then four years later Northumberland's Jim Alder won the marathon at the British Empire and Commonwealth Games in Jamaica. Almost continuously the North East had found a hero and then, as Alder's career trailed off in the late 1960s, along came Foster.

He was a promising school athlete who had headed to university in Sussex. Here though, his running suffered for two years when an iron deficiency problem was discovered in 1968. It was resolved, and with it his running career started to flourish again.

He made the English team for the Commonwealth Games with fellow Harrier John Caine, who was fifth in the 10,000m while Foster finished third in the 1,500m.

It was the first major medal in a career in which Foster became a star. Steve Cram, also Hebburn-born, could not help but be influenced. By 1978, the local pair were in the same English team at the Commonwealth Games in Edmonton and,

in Cram, the baton had a new holder. Cram progressed to an extraordinary career of his own – with three world records and gold in the 1,500m at the first World Championships in 1983.

Foster's career was moving towards its finale and he had been given an offer to run a marathon in New Zealand. He jumped at the chance.

The deal meant he could take his wife and two children with him and he could use the venue to stay on for three months to train for the 1980 Olympic Games in Moscow which was to be his farewell international appearance. He could never have imagined that by accepting this trip he would be taken on another journey from which he would never look back.

Having completed every Great North Run I have many happy and also sad memories of the race. The 1997 race took place two weeks after Princess Diana died and everyone was very emotional. I had a T-shirt printed with her picture and 'I dedicate this race to her' on it. Everyone I passed was clapping me – very emotional throughout the race. In 2003 one of my friends died just before the race. He used to run it every year. Radio Newcastle announced his sad passing just before the race and played 'Abide With Me'. We were all in tears.

My happiest race was when my daughter Caroline ran the race in 2003. She had just turned 17 and I think she was the youngest in the race. I was so proud of her.

Jim Broadbent
57, Retired, Newcastle-upon-Tyne

22 Peter Snell, of New Zealand beats Roger Moens of Belgium to win the Olympic 800 metres final, Rome, 1960.
23 Peter Snell wins the 1,500 metres at the Olympic Games in Toyko, 1964.
24 Steve Cram in action during the 1,500 metres final at the European Championships in Athens, 1982. Cram won the Gold Medal with a time of 3:36.
25 Brendan Foster gives the victory sign after equalling the World Record for 10,000m of 0:27:30.5 at Crystal Palace, June 1978.

STEVE CRAM *my part in it...*

Former World 1500m Champion now television presenter and commentator for the BBC.

ONE year I set myself a challenge, a bit of a bet, partly with the lads involved in the organisation.

My dad was running that year and I said I could watch the start and get to the finish before the leading athlete. Of course, if you have ever tried to get there through the Tyne Tunnel, it is impossible, and I had to take pictures to prove I was there.

I had this logistical exercise at the start, taking the picture, and then I jumped on the Metro

(which was fairly new then) and I got to the Four Mile point where I had pre-parked my car. I even lingered to take a picture of my dad before getting in the car.

As I know Jarrow and Hebburn well, I went bombing down some back streets, down a couple of illegal streets and it was going well until I got to the point of the Tyne Tunnel. I hit the incredible traffic and my only way of getting there was going across some waste ground between two roads, through this back street.

I parked my car about a mile-and-a-half from the finish and I legged it because I knew I had 7-8 minutes to make it. I reached the finish about 30 seconds before Mike McLeod, the leading athlete.

Ken Maling
opposite: Fairfax Suburban Newspapers Auckland

Chapter 2

RUNNING FOR FUN

WHEN Foster and his family boarded their flight to Auckland, he and the rest of the British Olympic team were in the middle of a difficult time preparing for the Olympic Games in Moscow, for which the participation of the British team remained in doubt. The USSR, the host nation, had invaded Afghanistan, and America had already threatened to boycott the greatest sports show on earth.

No decision had been made about Moscow, and for now those who wanted to be in the team had to ensure they kept fit. It was an awful chicken and egg scenario: train as hard as you can for an Olympic Games in which you might not be allowed to run.

At that time Foster was the Director of the Recreation Department at Gateshead Council where one of his main roles was staging major athletic events at the Gateshead stadium. His job did not deflect him from his running. By the start of 1980, however, his international career was heading toward its finale. He did not want it to peter out. He hoped that Moscow would be his final Games and he wanted to go there with the best preparation behind him. Fate played a part in taking him to New Zealand, coincidentally the country of his hero Snell, the man who had set him on his way 20 years earlier.

Since the mid-1970s, Foster had formed a great friendship with fellow runner David Moorcroft. They were both athletes of the highest standard and when he was not on the track, Moorcroft, the Coventry runner who went on to break the 5,000m world record in Oslo in 1982, had found the perfect combination of work and training.

Newly married, he and his wife Linda would spend English winters in New Zealand and he had often mentioned their visits to Foster.

As he winds the clock back, Moorcroft is perched behind his desk in Solihull near Birmingham. He is now one of the most powerful men in British athletics as Chief Executive of the sport's national federation.

"There was something about New Zealand that always fascinated me," he says. "They had such wonderful runners in John Walker (the 1976 Olympic 1,500m champion) and Dick Quax (a 5,000m world record holder) and I always wanted to go there to race.

"After the 1976 Olympic Games, a number of events were organised there for the start of the 1977 season. There were six races in 10 days, against the likes of Walker and Quax. I ran well and while I was there I met a former British Olympian, Vic Matthews, who was teaching in Hamilton.

opposite: Fairfax Suburban Newspapers Auckland
Frederic Lewis/Getty Images

"I went to his school and I was offered a job. I rang Linda and I took the position. I came back in September 1977 and I did not miss a year between then and 1988 and I used to tell Brendan about it."

Their friendship grew during the mid-1970s when Moorcroft, who is six years Foster's junior, was selected for the British team. He had first seen Foster as a fan, having travelled, as a 17 year-old, to watch him run at the Commonwealth Games in Edinburgh in 1970.

Moorcroft recalls: "By the following year I raced with him and by 1972, I knew him a bit. But it was not until 1976 that we actually spoke! It was when we were at Crystal Palace for the Montreal Olympic trials.

"Brendan had won the 5,000m and I was warming up for the 1,500m. He wished me well. I told him I was scared stiff. He replied: 'Yes but just think how you will feel if you are watching the Olympics on television at home in a few weeks' time when you could have been there competing.'

"That stuck with me. My race began, Steve Ovett won it – waving to the crowd – but I was second and made the team. What Brendan said might just have made the difference for those next four vital minutes of my running career."

Moorcroft was knocked out in the heats in those Olympics, but his friendship with Foster grew and by the time of the Commonwealth Games in Edmonton in 1978 – with Moorcroft as an established teacher in New Zealand – the pair became firm friends.

Moorcroft remembers the impact Foster had on him then. "We were there a long time and there were many diversions that could distract you from your event. Many people were over-training and Brendan held me back. He was very good at keeping me focused and ultimately we became the gold medal room. He won the 10,000m and on the day of the 1,500m final he told me that I too could win – he meant it and I did, beating the great Filbert Bayi of Tanzania amongst others.

"We had just happened to share a room because the team management did not put people together who were in the same event."

They would chat about nothing and everything, but one subject they did talk about was New Zealand.

Eighteen months later Foster was looking for a suitable place to prepare for the Olympics but he did not want to be far away from home on his own because both his children were young. By chance, he was offered an opportunity to run in the Auckland Marathon. "The race promoter said he would pay the air fares for myself, my wife and my family," recalls Foster.

It was an offer he could not turn down and his thoughts turned to Moorcroft, who was already there, 79 miles away from Auckland in Hamilton. He made contact and Moorcroft found him a house near to where he lived, and on January 2, 1980, the Foster family headed to the other side of the world, passports in hand.

Fairfax Suburban Newspapers Auckland

I trained a friend for what was his
first half-marathon for the 2002 GNR.
He came to me in May that year to ask
my help to enable him to improve his fitness
for the Blind Soccer World Cup Finals
in Brazil in November. Dave Clarke was
then Captain of the England Blind Soccer
team. I entered him into the GNR as I had
run it about five times previously and this
gave him a goal to aim for. He weighed 17
stone in May and wanted to go to Brazil
at 15 stone. By race day he was 15.5
stone. I guided him through the race but
at about 11 miles he blew up and was
really struggling. However, we successfully
completed the race in 2 hrs 10 mins but
we had a bit of a fall-out after we had
passed the finish line. Dave accused me of
taking advantage of his disability by saying
that if I could have seen the finish line (at
what was 11 miles) when I first said that I
could, then he said that "I had the eyes of
a Hawk"!

Mission accomplished though!

Phil Kemp
47, Bank Manager, Luton

27-28 and 30 *It was the spirit of Auckland's Round the Bays race that captured Brendan Foster's imagination: The result – the Great North Run – which has since gone on to become the world's biggest half-marathon.*
29 *Crossing the Verrazano – Narrows Bridge : The 1979 running of the New York City Marathon inspired Chris Brasher to found the London Marathon, the running of which in turn captured the imagination of the British public.*
31 *1981 Dick Beardsley of the USA and Inge Simonsen of Norway cross the line together to win the London Marathon with a time of 2:11:48.*

The day of the local marathon arrived and Foster had agreed to go beyond his normal distance by running in the race. Never before had he completed more than 20 miles and at the finish, his family and friends were concerned. With a few hundred yards remaining, Foster came into view and he was mirroring what what British runner Jim Peters had famously done at the British Empire Games of 1954, when his legs could carry him no more, leaving him wandering all over the track.

Moorcroft, who had been pushing Foster's daughter Catherine in her buggy (she had her first birthday while they were in New Zealand), was worried and says: "Brendan was wavering all over the road. I thought he was doing a 'Jim Peters' and he was going to struggle to finish. But it was not the case. On the road, there were some old tram lines and he was trying to avoid them – or he claims that was what he was doing!"

Foster ran an impressive 2:15 – a more than respectable time for an athlete running over 26.2 miles for the first time – to finish fifth, behind the winner, Dick Quax. In an upbeat mood he recalls: "If I had trained for it properly, I might have run it a lot better. It was 90 degrees of heat. I started it with a bucket of ice cubes in the hat I was wearing."

The race promoter was delighted and he asked Foster and Moorcroft whether they would like to run for him in another race, this time as part of his corporate team. They said they would. He told them it was a fun run with a serious side. It would take place in March and it was called Round The Bays.

By now, Foster was enjoying being in New Zealand: away from the cold British winter and missing out on the daily speculation of whether Britain was going to send a team to the Olympics. In the back of their minds one question could not be escaped. Were Foster and Moorcroft training for nothing?

In those days, there was no rolling television news or internet. They kept up to date by reading the New Zealand newspapers. "We had to wait two days to find out the latest news from home and that included the football results!" says Foster.

In this time they became a part of the running community. Moorcroft was a member of Hamilton Harriers AC and Foster and he would train together, as well as doing his own training. "Brendan was doing mega mileage, and I was training hard, and for me it was wonderful to be with a guy like that and comprehend the severity of some of the sessions he would put himself through," says Moorcroft.

Moscow was the long-term aim – if the British government was going to allow it – but in the short term, the date in their diary was March 20, 1980, for The Round The Bays race, and the pair did not know what they were letting themselves in for.

The first running boom was in full swing by 1980 and it is generally perceived that it began in America, very much on the back of Frank Shorter winning gold for the USA in the Marathon at the Olympic Games in Munich in 1972.

Shorter's victory in the USA coincided with the publication of Jim Fixx's Complete Book of Running. The age of the jogger had been born. The number of runners in American road races increased from four million in 1976 to eight million in the mid-90s, figures that have grown past the 10 million mark in the early 21st century.

In 1970 Fred Lebow set up the New York City marathon, the first of many to spring up around the world. It was while running in New York in 1979 that Chris Brasher had the vision of bringing such an occasion to London.

Before then people in Britain did not jog, and those runners who were seen pounding the roads were looked on with curiosity, no matter how good they were. As Brendan's wife, Sue Foster, says: "When he was running, people used to laugh at him on the streets. There were very few people who trained for athletics."

Nowadays, wander along to the banks of the River Tyne in Newcastle or the Thames in London at any given lunchtime and you have to dart out of the paths of several of the huge number of joggers who are running there – many of whom will be training for the Great North Run or London Marathon.

Some twenty-five years prior to this modern-day scene, Foster and Moorcroft were continuing their training in Hamilton, where they too found themselves embraced by history.

In 1962, long before running became fashionable, the Auckland Joggers Club was founded by Colin Kay and the world-renowned coach Arthur Lydiard. The latter subsequently coached Peter Snell and Dick Quax, amongst many others, to glory. He lived for athletics and has been described as the man who invented jogging.

He died in December 2004, at the age of 87, while in America on a speaking tour. The millennium issue of *Runner's World* magazine named Lydiard as one of running's five most influential figures of the century. It's not difficult to see why.

Auckland-born Lydiard, a shoemaker, had played various sports into his 20s and he believed he was fit because of the regular exercise he took, although he never trained in an organised manner. When he was 27, his metabolism was naturally slowing and he was feeling lazy. A six-mile run with an athlete friend further demonstrated the effects of his fitness – or lack of it.

"My pulse rate rose rapidly. I blew hard and gasped for air. My lungs and throat felt like they had been scorched. My legs were like rubber. My whole body felt the effects of the run and the effort expended to get me to the end of it."

Lydiard watched how other runners trained. He saw many of them run themselves into the ground. He explained: "Long, even-pace running at a strong speed produced increased strength and endurance – even when continued to the point of collapse – and was beneficial, not harmful, to regular competition."

By the start of the 1950s Lydiard was New Zealand's top marathon runner but it was his coaching technique that became his forte. He would prescribe the virtues of mild to vigorous exercise for ordinary health and at the New Zealand Sports Hall of Fame in his home city of Auckland, there is a message for all to read. It states: "Like none other, Arthur Lydiard's philosophy of running touches everyone that pulls on a pair of running shoes. He devised the principles of training employed by leading coaches and athletes all around the world, in track and field and many other sporting spheres; he invented the simple exercise of jogging which has infected millions with its benign bug."

Quax said of him: "We recognise all the great surgeons who are talented people and do a marvellous job. But they're the ambulance at the bottom of the cliff. What Arthur did was get people out doing light jogging for their health and you can't put a figure on how many lives that has saved."

Ten years after Kay and Lydiard had established the Auckland Joggers Club, they created an event. It was called the Round The Bays Race, run over a flat course that follows the contours of Auckland's Waitemata harbour. It starts in the city on Quay Street and finishes on the waterfront in St Heliers.

The first run attracted 1,200 participants and has now grown to be one of the world's largest fun-runs with nearly 40,000 registered runners... and an estimated 70,000 participants!

In 1980, two of those, Messrs Foster and Moorcroft, became engulfed in one of the experiences of their lives.

As Foster says: "Prior to this race the most inspiring sight I had ever seen in athletics was the runners in the English National cross-country, who were lined up across the bottom of the park at Parliament Hill Fields. In those days, it was the biggest race in the country, 1,300 people charging across Parliament

Hill Fields. It was an iconic shot, like the horses coming up the hill at Cheltenham.

"The National Cross-Country took place in the English winter in mud and rain; this was a sunny, brightly-lit Auckland seaside. With an inspirational picture of 30,000 people running along the road, it made a huge impact on me. I had never seen anything like it.

"The atmosphere was wonderful, everyone was running along the seafront. But at the same time it was a shambles... some people were on roller skates, others on bikes. Dave and I ran like hell, but I was only 36th because so many people entered the race at whatever point they wanted to. It was chaotic, in fact it was amateurish. But the spirit of the whole thing was absolutely fantastic."

They were running in the same team as Quax and Walker, and Moorcroft adds: "Give ourselves credit, Brendan and I would have finished higher up if we had run like this at the national road relay but it did not matter because the whole atmosphere was amazing. We were both bowled over by it.

"It was an 8.4 km race. It was one of the few occasions where you were running with a mob of people because normally at that pace you would be at the front. We had made the mistake of starting at the start – others had started way in front of it!"

But then it happened. They were only two miles into the race when Moorcroft recalls the historic moment: "I was too knackered to speak, but Brendan was chatting away. As we were running, in this glorious free-for-all, on a wonderful sunny day, he turned to me and said: 'I am going to do this in Gateshead in the North East'.

"I said, 'That's a great idea, good on you,' and even then it became obvious that he would do it," says Moorcroft. "But it did not dawn on me that he was going to create a half-marathon. That was breaking new ground.

"He was talking about it before the preparation for the London marathon had been started but he seemed entirely convinced he could run an event for a large number of people. Maybe he was thinking of life beyond athletics? He is the sort of person that, if he is going to come up with an idea, then it might as well be a big one."

When they reached the finish of this spectacular course that swung around the coast of the west side of the North Island, they were again both stunned. On the seafront, there were barbecues everywhere and one giant party for a city consumed by a sporting occasion.

"The atmosphere was not too dissimilar to South Shields now on race day," says Moorcroft. "There

was just this great party at the end and most of the runners walked back to the start to get their gear. There was no provision made at the finish to get them back any other way. Again, it was fairly chaotic, but it was massively enjoyable."

Foster says: "I really thought we could match the whole feel of the event. It was right, it felt fantastic."

It was March and within days the Foster family returned home. Day by day the Olympics were drawing closer. He was counting the days to Moscow, taking one job at a time.

Although he had not made his idea of a race in Newcastle public, he had quietly spoken to the man who had many times been at his side. Not even Foster could keep this a secret from John Caine.

31

SUE BARKER
my part in it...

A former World number three tennis player, Sue presents world class sport for the BBC, including Wimbledon and other major events.

The Great North Run is a challenge to all. It doesn't seem to matter what standard of runner you are. Everybody runs against themselves and against the course. The elite runners set themselves targets and goals, but so do the inexperienced fun runners. This provides an almost unique event where people are genuinely competing at all levels and everyone seems satisfied because everyone wins. In fact I'm a little jealous of this – as a tennis player it's a win or lose scenario, whereas just finishing the Great North Run seems, to me, a victory – irrespective of your time.

Over the whole weekend it's great to see genuine stars such as Kelly Holmes in the Great North Mile and the superb African and European distance runners, but it's the fun runners that make it for me. Some of them come up to me and say 'I hated PE at school and I've never won anything but I love this run.' But you know, a half-marathon is a long way and finishers, whatever their time, seem to have huge self-respect.

The charitable element is also fantastic. There are so many different emotions wherever you look which sets it apart from the London Marathon where the tone tends to be more serious. Everybody has a different but valid reason for running and collectively they provide one of the most inspiring events that I cover.

CHRIS CHITTELL *my part in it...*

Actor with top TV soap Emmerdale (Eric Pollard).

"By God it feels more like a full marathon than a half one. I've done it now about nine or ten times and it never seems to get any easier. The great thing is though that everybody helps each other out along the way. There are all shapes and sizes of people running and we all encourage each other. I don't go for PB's or anything like that, just run against my own clock. It's all for a good cause anyway as I run as part of the Emmerdale/ TV Times team to raise money for Leukaemia Research. I'll be doing a few 10ks this year to get ready for this year's run. To sum it up in one word: - Electrifying!"

LIZ McCOLGAN *my part in it...*

One of Britain's greatest distance runners, 10,000m gold medallist at the 1991 World Championships in Tokyo.

It was always one of my favourite road races, well organised and one which I enjoyed because of the amazing atmosphere. I had three good wins there and the crowd both at the start, along the course, and then at the finish got behind me. I can always remember the shouts of "Liz – come on!", in each of my appearances.

It's a big race where there is excitement shown by all the fun runners taking part and even though I lost in my last one I will always take away good memories of it. The course is also a good one, allowing you to run fast even though there are some hills in it.

Winning a world title on home soil is always something any athlete will remember and I still do. It was just fantastic.

I never felt any pressure when competing, because of the relaxed atmosphere. At the start the elite runners mix with the fun runners and the banter is absolutely brilliant.

Mark Shearman
opposite: Roger Coulam

Bryn Lennon/Getty Images

TIME TO RUN

WE are sitting in the boardroom at the headquarters of Nova International, the company that Foster formed in 1988 and which now has the Great North Run, and numerous spin-off races that have emerged from it, as its main business activity.

"It has been an extraordinary time," says John Caine, the company's Director for special projects. "Brendan and I have worked together for over 30 years, we have known each other for over 40. We used to fight all the time and we have had some fierce rows over the years. But his ability to do big daring things, well what can I say about that?"

Each year, one of the common themes identified by runners competing in the Great North Run is the family atmosphere that it generates. It is one of the founding principles of the event and one which is reflected in the friendship between Foster and Caine.

It began in the summer of 1963 when they both joined Gateshead Harriers. On their first day Foster was 14, Caine nearly 16. Although both took part in the 1,500m, the pair did not often run together. Their running careers blossomed at different stages, as Caine quickly moved up to the 10,000m. He was a schoolboy champion while Foster emerged later when at university, where he studied chemistry. Caine went to Loughborough to study PE.

Foster went back to teach chemistry at his old school, St Joseph's in Hebburn, while Caine was teaching in North West Durham. But they remained active members of Gateshead Harriers, having both made the English team for the Commonwealth Games in Edinburgh.

In 1974, the Labour government decided to re-organise local government, with the smaller authorities being amalgamated into bigger local area government bodies. Gateshead Town Council became Gateshead Metropolitan Borough Council and, as the existing councillors were going to be replaced, they wanted to make use of the money they had saved, before the old council became absorbed by the new set-up.

They approached Gateshead Harriers who were in need of a new synthetic track at their stadium.

The current track was so bad that in the winter of 1973, when Foster was preparing for the 1974 Commonwealth Games, he had to travel to Edinburgh by train to do some proper sessions, something he was unable to do at home because the Gateshead surface was boggy. It was a cinder track and when it rained or snowed, it turned to mud. The decision was made to invest the money in a new track at Gateshead and it became a memorable farewell present.

John Williamson

The council reorganised. For the first time, they created a Parks And Recreation Department with an upgraded track in an area where athletics was genuinely popular. However, there was no-one at the helm who knew much about sport and recreation. Foster was therefore invited to apply for, and was given, a management position. He resigned as a teacher that summer, going to Rome for the European Championships, where he won the 5,000m, and then he returned as a local hero to start work.

Says Caine: "He had this new job, and he had this stadium with a new track as part of that job. The first thing Brendan wanted to do with the new track was to make something of it. He refused to accept the status quo. He wanted to make an impact."

Foster decided to stage the Gateshead Games on the new track. It was an unheard-of development

Back in 1981 I, like most others in the race, had never run a half-marathon and had little grasp of what was needed to complete the distance. The race started and I was carried away over the first few miles by the general surge of excitement. After about nine miles I struck up a conversation with a fellow runner who, after mentioning pleasantries - married, two kids, age 30 - said he had been training extremely hard, so much so that his wife and children began to think he must be the lodger, smoking magic mushrooms, keeping a mistress or just downright crazy! After another mile or so I was still feeling quite good, and as he began to tire I felt a glow of satisfaction that my little training was paying off against his huge effort. I then noticed his number was extremely low - something like 136 - which, as lower numbers were

supposed to indicate a faster expected finishing time, did not sit comfortably with the situation unfolding. Why had this runner, with an extremely low number, having done vast amounts of training and running in a respected athletics club vest, not sprinted, or at least slowly eased past me?

Reality shattered my dream as on further questioning he revealed that he was the Club Champion Shot Putter! Numbers had been issued to club members irrespective of expected times. At 6 foot 4 and weighing perhaps 20 stone he was totally unsuited to long distance running. I had been completely blinded by my own achievements and felt rather humbled.

F D Whitfield
58, Accountant, Darlington

In 2001 I was lying in bed watching the GNR. Being a Geordie girl born and bred, but living in southern England, I was inspired by the thought of running in my home city, especially across the Tyne Bridge. I got up and went to my Mam and Dad's and told them - having not run since I was at school (I was 39 then). My Mam immediately said that I was too old

to take up running but my Dad was great. He was all for it, and said the whole family would be there to support me. Well, I ran the race in 2002 and all my family were there - all except my dear Dad, who sadly died of a sudden heart attack just two weeks after I announced I was running. I have been back every year since for my Dad. Every year I

have introduced another new GNR runner. I am looking forward to running across that bridge again this year, for my Dad.

Julia Lines
41, Fitness Instructor, Bedfordshire

in world athletics. The international stars would normally only compete in London.

He went to the BBC to see if they would cover it. He told them he was planning to break the world record. He appreciated that all the big meetings took place in London and the BBC said thanks, but no thanks. Foster went straight to ITV – and they said they would cover it. Armed with a letter saying it would be sponsored – by television retail company Rediffusion – Foster was on his way.

And he wanted Caine there with him. "Brendan asked me if I could organise the meeting," he recalls. "I was a PE teacher at the time on six weeks holiday. I agreed – and I have being doing it ever since."

In fact, thirty-one years on from those Gateshead Games, the formula has stayed the same. Caine says: "Nothing fundamentally has changed in the system of putting on an event: idea – funding – television. Without that you have nothing. Yes it has become more sophisticated, with the marketing and the sponsorship, but the basics have not changed.

"Brendan put his reputation on the line. He went to the local media. He told them what he was trying to do, he gained some great publicity."

The day of the event arrived and Foster's race, the 3,000m, was the last of the meeting. It was to be the highlight of a great day.

Caine recalls one great moment not long after the start of the meeting itself: "Brendan had made me Race Director and a photographer, Tony Duffy, came to see me and said he had taken an historic photograph. He said he had been standing on the roof of the changing rooms and took a picture of the gates being locked with people being turned away. The place was jammed. People were spilling onto the track."

They were not disappointed. It was August 3rd, 1974, and Foster broke the world record, running a memorable 7:35.2. As Caine says: "The place went ballistic and Brendan never looked back."

One great memory stands out for Caine amid all the excitement and euphoria of the world record. "I had grown up as a kid running in all the local harrier leagues and road races," he says. "Bill Dewing was always the No 1 timekeeper in the area. He was always there. After Brendan broke the world record for the 3,000m, he came up to see me with his stopwatch. It was a conventional watch and he had not reset it. He told me it was the first occasion he had timed a world record."

The next day, the BBC were on the telephone wanting a deal with Foster for the following summer. There had been only one world record on British television that year and it had taken place on ITV. The BBC came to see Foster and he used the leverage of putting on an annual Gateshead Games for the BBC to further expand the running buzz in the North East. Instead of attempting to demand a huge rights fee, part of the agreement was that they also televised a cross-country meeting in the winter.

The summer was over and on September 1, 1974, Caine went back to teaching. It was not for long. Foster set about putting together his team to run his department and the first thing he wanted was a manager for Gateshead Stadium. In October, he invited Caine to apply for that job. They have worked together ever since.

Caine says: "We started putting on an international track meeting every summer which became more sophisticated each year.

"In 1977, the meeting was the first stadium in Britain to have the Ethiopians running. We had Miruts Yifter (who became Olympic 5,000m and 10,000m champion in 1980) and he took five seconds out of Steve Ovett in the last 300m of a 5,000m. It was a stadium record – 13 minutes, 20 seconds.

"Lasse Viren (the two-time Olympic 10,000m and 5,000m champion) ran in our cross-country event, but in those days one of the biggest problems was actually contacting the athletes. Whereas the fundamentals remain the same for staging a meeting, it is now so different when you want to ask people to compete.

"We could not rely on agents because there weren't any. We had to make contact with the athletes and their coaches themselves. You had to spend the summer tracking them down, phoning their hotels when they were running on the circuit and asking to be put through to their rooms and do deals with them there and then."

All the time, Foster and Caine were staging many other activities at the stadium. Stan Long, Foster's coach and advisor, was employed as jogging manager. They created a race known as the

Lunchtime 5km Handicap, a race which still takes place once a week. "The stadium just boomed," says Caine.

They even employed another young talent: Steve Cram. "I interviewed him when he was a schoolboy, and I gave him his first job working for us during his vacation," says Caine. "He then went to Northumbria University but because he had a contract with us, he automatically came to work for us every holiday."

By the winter of 1979, Foster was given leave to go to New Zealand in January of the following year for three months. When he returned, he was buzzing. He had the knowledge of how to stage a major event and now he had seen, in the Round The Bays race, an event to beat all events.

Eventually, Prime Minister Thatcher decided against an Olympic boycott. Foster went to Moscow, where he was 11th in the 10,000m. He retired after that, and returned to work, the summer came and went and by November, he knew the time was right to find a fresh athletics ambition. Armed with his idea from New Zealand, he put his plan for a race into action.

He made four phone calls: one to Caine, the other three to fellow running friends from Gateshead Harriers. Caine was aware of what was going on but the message to the others was succinct: "I have booked a room at the Five Bridges Hotel for next Tuesday," he told them. "I have an idea. I am not telling you what it is but please be there at 5pm."

Our Great North Run story began when Brenda and I worked together in a shop in Morpeth. We had watched Mike Neville on BBC's Look North promoting the run and both thought that this would be a good idea to get us fit.

At first we were rather self-conscious being the only women runners around the area, and started by running around Morpeth Common so that no one would see us. We then progressed to the road and with a bit of encouragement from Jim Alder entered our first training race before the run, which was the Newbiggin 'S' road race. The next race was to be the Great North Run about two months later on 28th June.

We turned up at the run not quite sure what to expect or if we would actually be able to complete the full 13.1 miles. We were totally captured by the whole event. Even with just 12,500 runners competing the support was overwhelming. We now had the running bug which to date we haven't managed to shrug off and are both rather proud of our achievement of having completed all 24 runs.

Aileen Straughan
43, Finance and Administration Officer, Morpeth

39 36,37,38 *Running, spectating or in a wheelchair, elite or fun runner, all take part in the Great North Run. Here, the elite women power away towards the expectant crowds that line Gateshead's dual carriage ways.*

SIR BOBBY ROBSON

my part in it...

Top football manager and coach of England, Newcastle and some of Europe's elite clubs.

I started the race with Peter Reid in 1999. My first reaction was to the starting gun. It was like a blunderbuss – a massive noise – but it started what was without question one of the greatest sporting moments of my life. I'm telling you it was absolutely spectacular, there were runners of all ages, sizes, colours, all manner of dress–they just kept on coming and coming and coming. I thought to myself, 'When will this ever end?' It's tremendous – it must have lasted fully twenty-five minutes. I thought the tarmac would have worn out.

I was so impressed with the whole concept of the day. People were running for their own physical and mental challenges, many were running for exceptionally commendable charities and for all sorts of personal reasons. I imagine that most of them must have put a lot of work into getting fit to run. I must say I was tickled pink to have been a part of it.

Later that morning we took the ferry and went to the finish. There I saw a lot of people finish – some in great condition, some flagging, some on hands and knees, but they'd all done it. It was wonderful.

Evening Chronicle and Journal Ltd
opposite: Roger Coulam

Chapter 4

ON YOUR MARKS

41

THERE is a general feeling that if Brendan Foster wanted to plan the Great North Run today, it would not happen.

The logistics of it all would seem impossible because, as much as the saying goes about 'no idea being a new one', in fact what Foster was creating in Britain was unique. The safety and security aspects alone would probably leave it dead in its tracks. What is more, the request for a motorway to be shut for no reason except for a race might not even make its way to the local traffic department. Yet, in 1980, all those difficulties still had to be overcome. Today we have satellite television, instant communication, internet access, GPRS, emails... and of course the mobile telephone. When the first race was being planned, the organisers had no communication. The man at the finish did not know that the race had begun. It was not exactly a case of 'Look out, there are 12,000 runners coming your way,' but it was not far off.

The Great North Run has two major landmarks – the spectacular vision of the Tyne Bridge which the runners pass over within the first mile and the finish by the coast of South Shields. As the race weaves its way into Gateshead, tucked away to the right of the runners, just before they reach the international stadium where Foster and Caine learned the basics of staging athletics events, is probably the most significant building on the course. Most runners would miss it, but it is now the Swallow Hotel and was then, in 1980, the Five Bridges Hotel. Room 320 was simply furnished and there was a plate of sandwiches and two cans of beer set out for each person. And not much else.

Foster arrived first. The host wanted to make sure the others were not kept waiting. The four people he had invited were friends from the Gateshead Harriers, and they had established a bond through their running. Foster knew how each of them ticked, how they worked, and how one idea would trigger another.

Foster knew the only way his plan to stage 'a race in Newcastle' would be possible would be to call on people such as these – people who knew the sport and people he could trust.

Between 1975 and 1977, Gateshead Harriers achieved a rare feat in domestic athletics. They won the National Cross-Country Championships and 12-Stage Road Relay Team Championships, two of the most prestigious competitions on the British circuit, three times in a row. It was unheard of in the sport in this country.

Foster was one of the mainstays of the success, along with the friends, who, one by one, came knocking on the door of room 320: John Caine, Max Coleby, Dave Roberts and John Trainor. This is the team that went on to develop the famous race. It all started at this first meeting in the hotel in Gateshead. Now, 25 years on, the occasion has been recreated.

They are all together again in the same room in the same hotel with the new name. The noise is so loud,

Ad Infinitum

and the laughter so constant, that no one is allowed to finish a sentence without another interrupting. "It was just like this back then," recalls Foster.

Coleby, now 58, worked for Darlington Council at the time, and turns back the clock. "When we arrived we did not know what it was all about," he says.

In between sandwiches and beers, they sat and listened as Foster told them about what he had seen during his three months in New Zealand, when he had run in the Round The Bays race and how he thought that something similar could be established on Tyneside.

Even 25 years on, Coleby can still recall Foster's face at the meeting. "You could see in his eyes the enthusiasm he had for the idea," he says. "He was bubbling about it. When Brendan gets locked into something, it generally happens."

Coleby's memory of the night is clear. He says: "I had not seen Brendan for a week or so, because

Until January 2003 I'd no intention of running at all let alone running a half-marathon. Middle-age spread had set in and after New Year I was my heaviest ever – time for change.

I started regular exercise at the gym and running round the lanes, lost weight and even entered some local races. After the second I didn't feel so well with a nagging headache and started dosing myself with aspirin. Suddenly there was blood where there shouldn't be! To cut a long story short, two months later I was operated on for bowel cancer. Luckily I had been diagnosed early enough. I was, however, left with a problem – an entry into the GNR in six weeks time, a body that had been chopped apart and a surgeon who believed I shouldn't be standing up let alone running 13 miles!

One week before the race he could see how determined I was and how much progress I had made and relented – he said I could walk it, so I decided I would. There was then mad, frantic action to persuade friends, family and colleagues to sponsor my effort – it was worth it as we raised nearly £5,000 in a week!

I managed my Great North Walk in just over three hours and didn't feel too bright at the end, but I've been back and run it since and will be there again this year. I do realise how lucky I am.

Allan Hunter

41 A more normal view of the Tyne Bridge in Newcastle's busy rush-hour.
43 (clockwise) John Caine, John Trainor, Dave Roberts, Brendan Foster and Max Coleby meet up 25 years after their very first meeting to reconsider how the first Great North Run came together

his track season had finished, and I was still in training. He called me to ask if I was free for a pint on Tuesday night. I guessed he was up to something and my first instinct was that it was typical of the bugger–his Tuesday night training was over but mine was not, so he had organised it for that night.

"One thing stands out above anything else from the meeting. Brendan had said he wanted to have a race in Newcastle, but never, ever, did we talk about how often the race would take place. If anything, it was going to be a one-off. But there was never a doubt that it would happen."

Caine interrupts. "The only given was that it was going to include the Tyne Bridge," he says. "That was some given," replies Coleby.

The mention of the Tyne Bridge probably summed up the heights they were heading for, and on reflection the daring of the whole idea. The Tyne Bridge was built in the 1920s, an engineering feat of immense proportion, and the major gateway for traffic between Newcastle and Gateshead. Tens of thousands of cars travel across it every day – and five guys in a hotel were talking about closing it. They did not know it at the time but the Tyne Bridge had been shut only once before – in 1928, when King George V officially opened it.

The race's name became one of the great topics of the night and after much discussion, the general consensus was that they might call it The Geordie

Shields, it would be around 8¾ miles. You could hardly have that."

After careful planning of the route, the distance was agreed; it was to be a half-marathon and it would take in the Tyne Bridge, part of a motorway, and finish by the sea in South Shields. In hindsight it was a first-class decision, as the half-marathon distance and the start and finish all help to give the event much of its allure.

Trainor, 57, who now works for Nike in Amsterdam, does not forget his North East roots – or that night how they worked from a blank template. He says: "We were planning this race but we had nothing to compare it with. It is funny how things work out."

Caine interrupts. "But we understood the concept," he says. "The New York Marathon existed, so it was not like it was totally alien to us and we had organised some small runs in Gateshead. The funny thing is it was always a case of how the run would work – it was never a case of how it would not."

As Coleby adds: "It seemed right from the start."

Not that the five knew where the start would be, but Roberts was the man responsible for that. He laughs now when he remembers why. "I was the youngest and they probably took that into consideration," he says. "But I did not mind. If you are given the start, then the problems would run away from you. At least that's what I thought would happen."

When he was invited to the meeting, he recalls: "I had a sense that something was happening. When we heard the idea, it was great. We all had jobs and it would mean working on the Run in the evening – but by the time we left the hotel we were really up for it."

They finished by 7 pm; in two hours the Great North Run had been set in motion. They had a finishing point in South Shields, they had the focal point of the Tyne Bridge, they had no definite name, no start, no runners, and, no permission from the police. Twenty-five years on, incredibly, the police still have not given their 'official' permission, but like the five men in room 320, they went with the flow and never looked back.

5,000. A choice which was made because of the obvious connections with the North East and with the thought that they might reach that figure with hard work. "But if we didn't, what then?" recalls Foster. "We could hardly change the name."

The jobs were handed out. Trainor, who worked as a schoolteacher, was given the duty of looking after the finish; Roberts, who also worked with Foster and Caine, was given the start; Coleby was put in charge of the route. Foster and Caine would oversee the operation.

While Coleby would look after the route, there was an initial problem. He says: "I remember we did not even know how long the race would be – which I suppose is something of a major issue! I know some of the guys thought that it did not matter, but I felt it was of real importance.

"Brendan was adamant that we would finish in South Shields on the coast, reminiscent of what he had seen in New Zealand. I knew that if you ran from the Tyne Bridge to the coast of South

ALASTAIR CAMPBELL

my part in it...

Former Press Secretary for Prime Minister Tony Blair.

I have done the GNR twice and, knowing Brendan Foster, I will have to do it again to celebrate the 25th anniversary. Also my three children have all done the Junior GNR which, like the real thing, has a great combination of 'proper' runners and kids who just want to be part of something big and special. The adults' run is a tough course, and there are parts of it – like the motorway stretch uphill – that can be a bit quiet and lonely. Also that last stretch along the front, despite the crowds, feels a lot longer than it looks when you come off the steep downhill canter into the final bend and see the flags fluttering down by the finishing line.

Both times I've done it, Brendan has arranged for a good quality club runner to run alongside me and keep me going. In the first year I did it, Brendan was also taking part. He had three or four pacers so I guess he must be three or four times as important as me. He beat me by just over a minute, but I got my revenge when I beat him by 0.0001 seconds in the Great Ethiopian Run. Oh all right, it was a dead heat.

Last year, with Brendan retired to the commentary box, it was celebrity chef Gordon Ramsay I had in my sights as we struggled along the sea front to the end. My pacer spotted Ramsey struggling even more about thirty yards ahead of us. He had slowed to a walk. "Come on," said my pacer, Graham. "Let's overtake Ramsay." We caught him up, by which time I was so knackered I suggested we run in together, at which point the chef's competitive spirit kicked in and he raced off to beat me.

My other abiding memory is of my first GNR which came on the eve of my second appearance at the Hutton Inquiry into the death of Dr David Kelly. I was so concerned at putting a foot wrong in the eyes of the judge that I took advice from lawyers as to whether it was a sensible idea to be seen parading around a fun run the day before I was effectively on trial. The lawyers said it was fine and possibly a good way of preparing as I would have lots of time for reflection as I went step by step around the course. It was good advice, and the niceness of the crowd on the route was a timely contrast to some of the nastiness swilling around parts of the media at the time. It was also a reminder of how some people just weren't

following it to the same extent as the Westminster village. As I struggled round a roundabout on a South Shields housing estate, an old woman yelled out encouragement: "Go on Mr Hoon, you can do it."

The next day, Brendan saw me on the news walking into the inquiry and texted me to say he thought I was hiding the stiffness well. "I recognise that walk."

The reason the GNR works is partly because it's well organised, but above all because of the spirit of those who take part, and that shared feeling of fulfilment that comes with crossing the line, even if behind the likes of Foster and Ramsay.

Michael Steele/Getty Images
opposite: Roger Coulam

Chapter 5

GETTING SET

ON leaving the Five Bridges Hotel that evening, the five men knew what they had to do. It remains one of the achievements of the Great North Run's creation that it was organised within seven months. Unbeknown to them, Chris Brasher and John Disley were forming the London Marathon at the same time and within similar time limits.

While Brendan Foster and friends were putting together what they thought would be the biggest race in the country, the event in the capital would grip the nation because it had television coverage. It was a full marathon and it was something the people of Britain had not experienced before, outside of the major athletics championships.

Foster was in the commentary box for the first London Marathon and he remains the only member of the BBC athletics team who has been involved 'on air' for all 25 races.

The events have become kissing cousins and are landmarks of the sporting calendar – the London Marathon has a regular date in April and the Great North Run follows on in September or October.

Back in 1981, one was in March and the other in June. But, if anything, the gap between them now gives both an even greater impact. For runners such as Paula Radcliffe, the marathon world record holder, London is often seen as the way to start her season in earnest while the Great North Run is viewed as the prime occasion to end the year.

Not that Foster had attracting world record holders in mind when he returned home that evening in November 1980. The meeting he called had confirmed everything that he thought was possible. He had seen the glint in the eyes of his four friends, the eagerness in their desire to take on roles, and the enthusiasm they all shared. Now for the hard part: convincing the powers-that-be that a half-marathon could take place starting in Newcastle, travel through Gateshead and end on the North East coast in South Shields.

Foster and the team expected that they would have to be at their most persuasive. By the time they returned in December to report back on their findings, it became clear that no-one, as yet, had stood in their way.

Max Coleby, who has been course director of the Great North Run since its inception, had been given the task of planning the route, assisted by John Caine.

A startling difference between the Great North Run and the London Marathon is their respective backdrops.

John Williamson

Wherever Brasher and Disley had selected to start the London Marathon from, they knew a course of 26.2 miles would feature enough famous sites to make the route spectacular. The Great North Run had a different landscape; arguably, it had only one major landmark – the Tyne Bridge – which had to play a key part in the course.

Such was the eagerness shown, that on the evening after they met, Caine jumped into his car when he had finished work and set about driving across the North East in different directions to see where 13.1 miles would take him – with his starting point being this landmark of North East England: the Tyne Bridge.

Caine says: "We had agreed about it being a half-marathon and we knew that Brendan had insisted on it ending in South Shields. But of course we could not do that if we started on the Bridge. It was time to explore all the options, putting the icon of the Tyne Bridge at the centre of where my car would take me. Over that next week, I drove from the Bridge in every direction and when the mileometer read the half-marathon distance, I would decide whether I had made it to a reasonable spot. It quickly proved that I had not."

Caine's journeys from the Tyne took him to Morpeth, but there was already a race that started there and ended in Newcastle. It was only 10 miles. Too short!

Next, he drove south on the A1 to Chester-Le-Street, but that direction had a pronounced uphill

After the completion of the 2003 GNR I was getting changed between buses 30 and 29 next to a friendly and distinctly less tired looking man. We exchanged the usual "How did you do's?", etc. I said to the man, "I recognise that accent, is it Cambs or Norfolk?" He said, "Wisbech in Cambridgeshire, you'll not know it!" I said "I DO know it, I was born there!" So the chances of that happening amongst 45,000 people are rare, but...

I went on to say "My dad was probably the only person to play 1st team football, cricket, rugby and hockey for Wisbech Town." The man said "You must be David Jenkinson's son then!" This fellow GNR runner was a former work colleague of my late dad's best friend Gordon Timm. I believe my dad will have been looking down on that cherished moment and he'll know how very proud we all are of him!

Jim Jenkinson
37, Regional Officer for YMCA, Rotherham

47 Calm before the storm. The South Shields Coast – a picture of peace.
48,49,50,51 As with other major sporting events, marquees, temporary grandstands and a plethora of people create a village for the weekend – the finish of the Great North Run is no exception.

crossing it and heading towards Whitley Bay.

"It did not have the right feel to it, and of course it did not have a finish on the coast in South Shields," explains Caine. "I was trying out all the options, before deciding to go east towards Shields to see where the required 13.1 miles would take me."

He took a diversion and reached South Shields with his mileometer on only 10 miles.

"It wasn't by the coast or anything," he says. "It wasn't right. Then I drove on, and made the dramatic drop to the seafront. The impact of doing that hit me. 'Wow!' I thought to myself. I had this big stretch of road in front of me, and as I was driving along it, the miles were inching up. It reached 12 when I ran out of road, so I decided to turn the whole idea upside down."

He pulled his car over, parked, jumped out and looked back along the road from where he had just driven.

The waves of the North Sea were crashing against the beach, there was a cool evening breeze and for a second he imagined a race taking place. He was standing on the pavement by the side of the huge banks of grass that separate the beach from the road and he thought of that as the finish – now the task was to trace back the route he had just driven and see where it took him.

The one criterion he had was to go over the Tyne Bridge. He ended up on the motorway section of the A1 that leads out of Newcastle. The route of the Great North Run would end where its creator would want it to and it would pass over the Tyne Bridge. But now the task had become tougher.

While they had known they would have to ask the authorities to close the Bridge, they would also need to shut a motorway. The persuasive powers of Brendan Foster would need to be working on overdrive, though as Caine adds now: "Looking back, it was amateurish the way we were doing things."

Caine and Coleby were in constant touch about the route before they met again in December.

Coleby was making plans for the half-marathon, irrespective of where it was going to start and finish, by working out who he would need to assist in staging the race. It brought him his most often-told story of the run.

The numbers they had anticipated for the first race were around 5,000 and they knew that they would need medical support, so Coleby travelled to meet the director of the local Red Cross. He left with her full support–and in total bemusement.

He says: "I told her of our plans and how we were all fired up for the race and how we thought we might be able to attract 5,000 people to run in it. I thought I needed to give her all the information I could to convince her that we needed the help of the Red Cross and how they would be required at every mile point to assist. She did not say a word, but then looked back at me and asked one question: 'Why?'

"I was astonished. I did not know what to say. Of course they would help, of course they would do what they could, but what she could not comprehend was why 5,000 people would want to run 13.1 miles – and then simply go home after it. No-one had heard of such an idea."

Generally, discussions went well. He says: "People might think that there were stumbling blocks along the way but we did not have anyone actually saying they didn't want to get involved or help because the idea was so exciting."

It was a time-consuming preparation. Along the course they would need drinking stations, so he spoke to the fire brigade about using the water hydrants on the road. It was not their decision – so they directed him to the local authorities who gave him permission, and to Northumbrian Water who provided the manpower. But then who would man the watering stations? He thought of the Scouts, and in every run since then helpers from South Tyneside and Gateshead Scouts have been integral parts of the race's success. They remain among the unsung heroes.

When the five gathered again at the Five Bridges in December 1980, Coleby presented the meeting with six sheets of A4 paper, reporting back his findings of how the route would be manned, how the willingness was being shown in abundance and how it would cost around £750 for all the minor things that would make up such a major occasion, such as buying cups for the runners to put their water in – no such thing as handy-size water bottles back in 1980. Every contingency was being considered.

Foster was making inroads into the promotional side, and, back at the Five Bridges, the run was into its opening strides... but they did not want to rush. They were looking for a date and they selected it in the simplest and most obvious way. They looked at the athletics calendar for the year and chose the final Sunday in June, the 28th. It was a day that did not clash with any other athletics event in Britain – yet, as Foster recalls, would it have mattered? It was only going to be a local race with a few thousand people...

The conversation was slightly more serious at this second meeting because the race plan was gaining

significant momentum, and the issue of its name was raised again – if they were to attract more than 5,000 for a run called the Geordie 5,000, what would they do?

The five men sat and contemplated. Other suggestions were made – from the Tyne Race to something as simple as Newcastle-Shields when Caine had a thought.

He recalls the story: "My mind was wandering and I remembered the time when I was in my 20s that I hitch-hiked home to Newcastle from Nottingham. I did it all the way along the A1– which goes by another name of the Great North Road.

"I said to the guys: how about the Great North Run? Just like that."

They had it. The Great North Run. It summed up everything that they were aiming for. They wanted a race, but they wanted a run for the people.

They did not want it to sound too elitist and this name was perfect: a race implies winning, a run implies taking part.

They wanted to encapsulate the area, and this it did. They wanted to convey what they were trying to achieve–an event on a big local scale and the word 'Great' summed that up.

1982

On the 2nd of April 1982, Argentina's military government launched an invasion of Britain's colonial possessions in the South Atlantic and for a few short months world attention was focused on the tiny Falkland Islands. By June Port Stanley was back in British hands, but the victory cost the lives of 255 British Servicemen and nearly a thousand Argentines died in the conflict. Closer to home, however, there appeared to be no light at the end of the Cold War tunnel with the news that 96 American cruise missiles would soon be based on British soil. This led to a revival of the previously dormant Campaign for Nuclear Disarmament and the setting up of a permanent 'Peace Camp' by the entrance to the US airbase at Greenham Common. Yet if the gulf between East and West seemed as wide as ever, one centuries-old conflict did come to an end: in May 1982 Pope John Paul II made his historic visit to England, the first by a pontiff since The Reformation.

ALAN SHEARER
my part in it...

Former Captain of England and Newcastle United's current Captain and leading goalscorer.

IT was a great honour to be asked to start the race. At the time I had my ankle in plaster – I'd been injured in a pre-season match. It seems to have been going for years. I remember when I was a kid, people used to talk about it then. It's a massive event now, one of the biggest in the sporting year, and great for the North East – look at the number of people that take part and spectate. At the start, when you stand up and watch thousands of people running past you – it just seems to go on and on. It's amazing!

I went to the finish later and my impression was one of relief. I was just glad I wasn't doing it! It's not just a great day now, it's a great weekend with the build up starting on Friday – it's a real occasion.

I might do it one day. I can't now because it clashes with the early season – but one day, maybe.

Owen Humphreys/PA/Empics
opposite: Roger Coulam

READY TO RUN?

THEY liked the idea of the route that Coleby and Caine had worked out; but they were not quite sure whether starting it on the motorway would work. The option of Northumberland Street, one of the prime shopping areas in Newcastle, was discussed. They thought that if they began the Run outside the Odeon Cinema, then the runners would be able to change there before the race. It was an idea floated, but one which disappeared once the entries started rolling in. The Odeon would not be big enough.

But they continued to explore all the options. The priority now being how to close the Tyne Bridge, something that had never been done since its official opening in 1928. What they did know was that the road was sometimes closed for maintenance work. Coleby and Caine were put on the case.

Coleby explains: "It really just happened; we never put it down as an agenda item – and neither the council nor anyone else ever questioned it. We just agreed that we wanted the race to go from the motorway in Newcastle to South Shields. We never once made a big issue about the Bridge and neither did anyone else; as a result, its consequent closure never became a stumbling block".

Their enthusiasm was high when they gathered again. "It was working," says Caine. Well, almost. By the time of that next meeting they knew Brasher was developing the London marathon, which was potentially a great plus, but they had also found a stumbling block. The police had not agreed to close the roads.

Foster handed out copies of a letter which he had received from Northumbria Police that could have put an end to the idea. He had written to the Chief Constable, Sir Stanley Bailey, and the reply read: "With reference to your letter of recent date, it is not my policy to encourage sponsored events on the highway in view of the obvious danger to all concerned. If, however, you decide…"

At 68, Terry Rutherford has been long retired from his position as Chief Sergeant with Northumbria Police, but each year he watches the Great North Run and chuckles at the same time about what happened back in 1981 when the police force had come up against an unstoppable force in Foster.

Rutherford says: "We received this letter from Brendan Foster saying he was thinking about having a road race but little did we know how big a race he was talking about.

"For events on the highway, he received the standard reply telling him that it was not our policy to agree – and what happened? The run grew from there."

The Highway's authorities had agreed to the closures but there was no way Foster could have an event of this size without the support of the police. The prospect of 5,000 runners with probably double the number of spectators – again an estimated guess – would need to have some official police presence.

Rutherford adds: "Brendan Foster has a tendency to make things happen first and then tell you what is going to happen. Our letter might not have endorsed the idea but soon it became obvious that it was going to become a big local event, it was going to create enjoyment and pleasure, and it was going to take place – and take place on roads in this area – so the police had to get involved."

Despite this, they never wrote back to Foster to give their agreement and still they have not actually told him officially that they are happy for it to take place. But each year they have been there supporting the biggest weekend of the year in the North East.

As Rutherford says: "But not everyone was happy. We were apprehensive, principally because no one had any idea of the sort of problems that that number of people on the roads would bring. We had not seen anything like it before. Brendan knew from New Zealand that it could work but there was quite a lot of opposition to be overcome. The police needed to consider the manpower required and other safety aspects.

"The local football matches were probably the biggest thing in the area in terms of crowd control but this race required different aspects to be considered – how would it affect the rest of the community, for example, whose roads would be shut on the day of the race. It was also troublesome because of the manpower involved. There had to be a lot of attention paid to those who were not taking part, the isolated communities. But Brendan is a good publicist. Once started it was like a rolling stone. You could not stop it."

Even though the police had not given their official permission, every other element had fitted into place by the third meeting.

They had a name, they had a route, they had people to help out on that route, they had water to give the runners, they had permission to close roads, they had a date, they had the Tyne Bridge and they had the finishing line by the coast that Foster had considered essential. But they were missing one rather important ingredient – they had no runners. They did not have to wait long.

John Bird was the editor of the local evening news programme on BBC called *Look North*. It was the top news show in the region and it was presented by Mike Neville, the area's biggest television

1983

The year's big film was Return of the Jedi, the third in the original Star Wars trilogy, and back on earth science fiction seemed to be becoming science fact with a host of technological innovations. Apple Macintosh launched Lisa, the first computer to use a 'mouse' and drop down menus while Tandy revealed the world's first battery powered portable PC and coined the word 'laptop' to describe it. In Europe, electronics company Phillips introduced music lovers to the compact disc while Sony capitalised on the success of their Walkman (that essential jogging aid) with a pocket TV called the Watchman. Less peaceable technological firsts came from US president Ronald Reagan and his proposals for a 'Strategic Defence Initiative' that would use space-based satellites and lasers to shoot down nuclear missiles; inevitably the policy was soon dubbed 'Star Wars'.

53,54,55, *The BBC team have pride of place overlooking the finish, while some distance away a tented village is created for the many charities to entertain runners who have run and raised a small fortune for them.*

personality. The pair knew Brendan Foster well. Based on friendship, trust and a desire to help, it was a combination that could not fail from the moment Foster and Bird discussed the idea.

"I remember Brendan ringing me to ask for our help in something he wanted to promote," recalls Bird. "He thought I could help. It sounded good."

Bird has now been retired from the BBC for thirteen years but the Great North Run remains one of the most memorable projects that he ever worked on. If it was not for the contribution made by the BBC's offices in Newcastle, the race might not have happened. But it did; the willingness for success spread wherever you looked.

Foster needed no introduction to the people at the BBC – he had been a regular guest on their shows as his fame and success had grown during his running career. He knew this programme could give his race even greater credibility. At 6 pm each night, *Look North* would run for half an hour. The audience watching Neville was bigger than all their network rivals.

Bird says: "Brendan was an international athlete who had put the North East on the map. He had been on television so often and one day he just came into my office and said he had seen this amazing race in New Zealand and that something similar could be a winner here in the North East.

"He told me he wanted to organise it, but wasn't sure how to get the publicity. I told him we would be delighted to promote it. As we chatted, we thought between us that we would get around 3,000 runners; in the end, it became a nightmare!"

From five friends, it became seven as Bird and then Neville joined in the fun.

Foster went on air to announce that the Great North Run would take place on June 28th and it was anyone's chance to take part. He proceeded to appear on the show virtually every night for weeks on end, promoting the race. The response was amazing.

Neville loved having Foster in – because all the time there were new aspects of the run that they could chat about. He says: "Brendan was THE man in the 1970s. I remember in 1977, I went to cover an event in Atlanta and Brendan gave me a pile of T-shirts to take with me – with the 'Gateshead For Sport' motif on. I gave them to the people I was staying with. My hostess, Linda was wearing the T-shirt when we were filming one day and a lady came up and asked us: 'Excuse me, what is Gat-es-head?'

"I told her all about Brendan and then Linda explained. When he was in the Olympics, people who had no interest in running became interested.

We got on so well. We were pals. When John mentioned the idea for the race and about Brendan coming on to the show, it sounded tremendous."

So there it is: total co-operation once again from a prime source.

Such was Bird's enthusiasm that he decided the BBC would handle the entries and that viewers would write in to BBC North to apply for an information pack. They would then return it with their race entry – which the BBC would process and send back. Easy? Not quite so.

Neville says: " As soon as it was announced, there was a buzz in the air. Everyone got so deeply into it. We trailed it every night... Brendan would come in and provide the latest updates – from the prizes people would receive to what time the race would start."

The local public had been caught up by the occasion and then, on March 29, the London Marathon took place; 24 hours later the BBC had never experienced anything like it.

The entries had been growing each day, but once the public had seen what a mass participation race was all about, they wanted to be in something similar. And where was the next race?... The Great North Run in Newcastle.

The London Marathon proved to be everything that the Great North was building towards – an occasion rich in emotion, sentiment and wonderful stories. It had elite runners but it was not all about times and performances. It was about the club runner and the fun runner competing on a route they would never have known before. London caught the public's imagination because it was the classic distance of the marathon entwined with the history of the capital city.

And on a rain-soaked day, a finish that could not have been scripted. Rarely has there been such camaraderie in a major sporting event as that shown at the finish by Dick Beardsley of America, and Norway's Inge Simonsen, who crossed the line together in first place – hand in hand.

It had 7,747 starters, it had a men's race with a fairytale finish and the women's event saw Joyce Smith, 43, of Britain, break the national marathon best time. Inspirational stuff, along with those who were running the distance for the first time.

The country was gripped and the next night Foster, who had been an integral part of the BBC's commentary team for the London race, was back in the studios of *Look North* – telling the people of Newcastle that in 12 weeks' time, that could be them. And what a good choice it had been to have the Great North Run as a half-marathon. It would

The Great North Run of 2001 was the furthest distance I had ever run in my life and I was not at all certain I could do it. I had several hundred pounds worth of charity money riding on the outcome and I drove up to Newcastle with my wife on the Saturday, anxious but excited. The two and a quarter hours that followed on the Sunday morning were amongst the most exhausting and exhilarating I have ever spent. I felt inspired to capture the mood of the day in a poem:

I.
Saturday afternoon before the Race
Gridlocked all the way to Jesmond –
Estates, motorbikes, caravans and trailers
All edging closer to B&Bs and friend's settees,
Before checking out routes, start lines, portaloos,
Restaurants, phone boxes, weather news.

II.
The evening before the Race
Newcastle City Centre, spilling over
With jubilant Geordies waxing lyrical, in clover
Over late winners against Manchester United;
Vying with small groups in tracksuits, visibly excited
As they jostle and walk faster
To queue outside anywhere selling pasta.
Back home in the room – staring at the ceiling
To the engine drone of the fridge;
Giving way to eventual dreams of sprinting across
The curving Tyne Bridge.

III.
The morning of the Race
Following the seasoned press short cuts,
Across fields and past boarded-up groundsmens' huts.
Deep breathing to appease the flutter
Of butterflies hurtling like deflated balloons.
The stripping away of tracksuits, before the long stretch
To the back of the queue. Regretting that everyone knew
About the surprising warmth inside a bin-liner.
Killing time with a bloke from Ipswich, as Steve Cram
jokes about the lack of Man U shirts in the crowd.
(A few Newcastle fans laugh out loud).

IV.
The start of the Race
A minutes silence; stars and stripes held
Stretched over bowed heads. A frosty fear weds
Itself into each runners' hips, like the track tingling
Approach of an intercity. The unison countdown
And the starter's gun...
Followed by absolutely nothing, as Ethiopians
and Moroccans run
Off into the distance, while we stand and wait,
jogging on the spot, (PBs already ticking away)
Until the painfully slow pubcrawl to the line and the wave
To the cameras as the pace quickens and we try to save
A half-decent time, before it's really too late.

V.
The first half of the Race
We pass under the flyover, (while men stop to pee -
Having taken stocking up on water too far) then we emerge
To pavements thickly spread with cheering crowds,
As we stream past, grinning - almost in a dream.
Moving, adrenaline-fast, straight through
Dual carriageway traffic lights without the tedium
Of turn-taking or the chancing of amber.
Each mile brings another band - bagpipes, electric
Guitar, steel and samba - raising spirits, surging
Us forward, along with the clapping bystanders,
Until we reach the long, silent stretch of the motorway.

VI.
The second half of the Race
Thousands of apple-bobbing heads ahead,
A swarm of human traffic, all homing in
On South Shields and all that matters.
Eight, nine, ten miles come and go:
Celebrities are pulled out to mention their latest show.
Motivators with microphones call out mile-counters
With the urgency of hyped-up Bingo callers.
My pace slows further as we swerve into the suburbs,
Through council estates of betting shops,
Everything-For-A-Pound basement bins, newsagent
Peddling scandal for small change and
Pigeon-smattered statues to nobody special.
An old woman offers me chunks of melon
In her weekend hand; her timing
Could not have been better planned.

VII.
The end of the Race
At the end of the town inches a slow incline
All along which you can almost sense the finish line
With each treacle-sodden step. Time pulls you back
With the pain of feet pocked with blisters -
But fear of failure is a far greater ache
Than the passing chill of gruesome fumes, which passes,
Almost as soon as the popcorn is digested.
Alex takes my photo as I approach the final straight,
Cooked by the sea-breeze and running on dregs.
I cross the line, elation and relief blurred
In an exhausted and shameless delirium -
Beautiful and vague; like the contours of parked cars
The morning after a heavy snowfall.
In the Heavens it reads:
Two hours, seventeen minutes and thirty two seconds.

Andrew Dethridge
Sunderland

---

mean a variation on a very successful theme. The outcome...mayhem.

It had been decided that the BBC would administer all the entry forms which had been printed in *The Journal*, Newcastle's morning daily newspaper. Foster knew the editor Phillip Crawley well, and what Crawley did next was one of the most important decisions of his career.

Now 60, his professional life has taken him across four continents and he is now publisher and Chief Executive Officer of *The Globe & Mail*, Canada's leading national newspaper. He originates from Gateshead, where Foster had become a hero at the Harriers, and back in 1981, he sensed the race could be a winner. Crawley explains: "The day we carried the entry form, was one of the greatest gambles of my early professional career. It was a question of how many copies of the paper do you print.

"When Brendan first came to me with the idea, he already had BBC North East interested and he wanted to get the newspaper involved because he realised that this would be part of the promotional build-up which was necessary to create awareness and encourage public participation.

"These were the days when mass fun runs were not well known concepts in the UK. At *The Journal*, however, we had a long tradition of being associated with road running because we sponsored the annual New Year's Day road race between Morpeth and Newcastle. At the time that attracted about 250 people. Brendan came along and said that we could create this big fun run and make it into something that really appeals to people as well as getting them fit and active and what he wanted to know is could the newspaper become involved?

"Our job was to carry the entry form in the newspaper. You had to fill in the form and send it back (to the BBC). "I had to ask myself, how many people were going to apply? Was it going to be 5,000, 15,000, 25,000? How many copies should we print? You do not want to print too many – but you do not want to be caught short.

"It was not a big selling paper, with a circulation of about 70,000, so I persuaded the powers-that-be, that there would be great interest and they should be ready to extend the print run. We sold an additional 50,000 papers that day!

"In terms of a single one-off circulation coup for the newspaper, it was a fantastic success. Thinking back on it, I now think, 'My God.' I probably took my career in my hands. If it had flopped and we had wasted huge money on newsprint, I would have been a very unpopular man."

Within 24 hours, the BBC local office was bombarded, in fact overwhelmed, with letters from people wanting to take part.

"It was astonishing," says Bird. "We had received quite a few entries before then but now they just started flooding in. *Look North* covers right down to North Yorkshire and in those days it also went across to Cumbria, up to the Scottish borders. In addition Brendan had many other connections, and by word of mouth, it gathered momentum within and outside the area. We had 20,000 applications in that first year!

"Day after day the bags were piling up, we could hardly open the front door of the offices because people had shoved entries through the letter box. We had to call in extra staff, from Brendan's wife and John Caine's wife to more staff at the BBC. But there was a family spirit within the BBC and that is how it worked. Everyone pulled together, from Tom the doorman to my secretary. It is something that none of us will ever forget. We did not expect it would be such a problem, but in the end, my secretary had the worst of it."

As now, almost a quarter of a century later, Jean Williamson recalls:

"We used to arrive for work and there would be queues of people outside the building," she explains. Now 67, of Rowlands Gill, she has retired from the BBC after 22 years but remembers that: "It was amazing. The people wanted to ensure their letters got there - so they delivered them themselves.

"We had to call on other people for help, such as the girls in the newsroom, other secretaries, who all had their own jobs to do but in any spare moment, they would be on hand to assist. We also had to find a place for the mailbags. We decided to use the Green Room which was for our guests appearing on the show – and John's office became the temporary Green Room.

"In the end people had to work full time on the entries and I had a list of casual workers who would do the occasional shift who we called in to help. It became such a thing that one of the local newspapers had a photograph of me sitting in the middle of these sacks because there were so many of them. We developed a system…

"We had long benches where all the bags were put. The envelopes were slit open, put into a box and the process repeated again and again. Brendan was naturally really interested in what was happening and how many application forms we were getting. Even though he and John Caine were busy organising the race, they were very much hands-on."

Bird says: "Mike Neville was one of the most popular people in the North East but Brendan brought them out from their houses. He encouraged people to get fit in a way no-one had previously done. It was the beginning of people running to get fit. Whenever you went on the roads, all you could see were joggers. Early in the mornings, late in the evenings, all age groups. People up to the age of 80 were taking part."

They were all writing in – and the race had become the talk of the town.

The biggest topic was the number of applications. What were they going to do with 20,000? Thankfully, they had not called the race the Geordie 5,000 because there would have been quite a few disappointed people.

As the race was in its infancy, they had to put a limit on. But as Bird says: "Who do you put in and who do you leave out?"

They agreed on a figure of around 12,500 after consultations with all the relevant authorities. All this time the BBC was provided with a range of different stories which further publicised the run-up to June 28th.

It was a similar story in another part of Newcastle. Sue Foster explains: "In the early years the race was run by just a small group of people. It was run from our dining room table at one point.

"People would send in their cheques for their entries (a fee of £5 had been asked to cover administration) and I can remember going to the bank with carrier bags full of cheques, paying them in individually."

May 1st. The closing date for the race and entries had become like gold dust. It seemed people would pay a fortune to be part of the race – and one man did. Bird had been invited to a Sports Aid Foundation dinner. He had an entry to the Great North Run but he could not run in it because he was covering the race for television on the day. He decided to auction the entry at the dinner... and it was bought for £400.

58, 59 The Start: As the 45,000 plus runners assemble, some take it easy but the buzz builds and soon turns to fever pitch.

MARK KNOPFLER *my part in it...*

Guitarist, vocalist and songwriter for Dire Straits and more recently a best-selling solo performer.

I remember marvelling at the sheer number of people. All shapes and sizes, some of them not the sort you would expect to be able to run for a bus, let alone a half-marathon. The collective motivation and the individual dedication was amazing.

I am used to high pressure big events but I was really impressed by the level of organisation and coolness of those in charge. Brendan Foster seemed very together and focused. Sue Barker gave a perfect live introduction for the BBC. I also remember talking to one of the runners, Alistair Campbell, who had a lot of bad media attention at the time but he showed no sign of the pressure getting to him.

I had to share the starting duties with John Motson who, unlike me, was running the race. We had to fire the starting pistols and so were introduced to the marksman – a guy dressed in a bright red bomber jacket. He gave us very strict instructions. When he gave the word we had to raise our weapons, on his say-so fire them and then discharge them in an orderly fashion. In the actual event – we raised our weapons and waited for his signal. Nothing came – eventually he shouted: "Well go on then!". We let off a ragged volley then John just threw his pistol to the ground jumped off the rostrum and joined in the race. All protocol discarded. We had let loose this torrent of people – it seemed like hours before they all ran past, being urged on by the frantically excited commentator.

Sights such as the soldiers carrying their full packs and a guy in deep-sea diving gear really stick in my memory for their show of strength and determination.

When the final person had gone past I felt strangely alone and left out. I didn't really know what to do. I would like to take part one day – it must be an amazing sense of achievement.

Bryn Lennon/Getty Images
opposite: Ad Infinitum

Chapter 7

GO, GO, GO

SONIA O'SULLIVAN

my part in it...

One of Ireland's greatest ever athletes. In 1994 and 1995 World and European title holder and nine times Grand Prix winner.

IT is one of the greatest races because it is about far more than just the Run itself. So much surrounds it. Since 1998 when I saw everything that goes on around it, it has changed so much every year and it has become bigger and better and something that everyone wants to do. You will be missing out if you do not run it.

Every year I think I'm not sure I'm going to make it to the Great North Run and then every year I do. I always remember watching it on television, when Liz McColgan used to run, and thinking that it looked like a good thing to do.

The first time I entered, in 1997, I did it as a training run, but the second time was the first time I had run a half-marathon seriously and I wondered: 'How am I going to do that?'

There is something about the roundabouts. When you are coming towards them, the music starts to play louder, it makes you run a bit faster, and it spins you around it and off the other side.

Around 10k, you come to a roundabout and you think you are going straight and then you make this sharp left hand turn. All of a sudden, the wind gets behind you and you fly down the road and you feel like you are heading to the sea.

The worst thing is that if you have the wind behind you the whole way, you are guaranteed to have the wind against you in that final mile – and you have to weigh up which you would rather have. It is one of the hardest miles to run. They have a flag or camera in the distance and it seems so far away. There is even a hill in it. It seems to go on forever.

I think word of mouth is important to the growth of the race. Many people do it with a group of friends that gets bigger every year, as more people want to be involved, and the quality of running at the front improves too.

Getty Images

John Williamson

63 Across the course the a
buses glide down a series of roads which are all closed for 13 plus miles.   eet of

FOSTER could not quite believe the response there had been, from far and wide, as well as from people in the North East. The event, for which they had anticipated a field of 5,000 runners, had rapidly exceeded that number and had become an even greater logistical operation.

Between Foster first appearing on *Look North* in February, and the race day of June 28, the team called on as many of their friends as they could to help out. In the run-up to the race they met with police, the local councils, the traffic management divisions and the medical and fire services, all keeping in touch with each other as plans progressed.

The excitement was immense, as was the pleasure of putting together an event that they knew would capture the imagination of the North East. "I can never remember Brendan letting it get to him," says his wife. "There was no occasion that he was up at night worrying about it. In fact, he has never done that in all the 24 years of the race."

He had great trust and faith in the people he had put in charge of the key jobs.

Max Coleby was crucial in setting up the 'services' that would operate on the course, but he also had a great interest in course measurement away from the race. It was his responsibility to measure the exact route of the Great North Run, the 13.1 miles that would start on the A167 (M) and end

at South Shields. It was a stop-start operation – and on certain stretches he needed access to the road itself to check the distance.

Coleby had been in contact with the police who said they would provide him with two motorbike escorts. But that would have to be on a Sunday morning – a day when he should be training. His coach, Alan Storey, did not want him to miss a session because Coleby was among the country's leading marathon runners and was a British International.

He takes up the story. "Alan was concerned that I would be missing a training run, while the police wanted us to start at 5.30am, a good time because there would be little traffic on the roads. I came up with a solution. I suggested to Alan that if I ran the course, he could cycle it at the same time and do the measuring! He agreed. We had two police motorcyclists with flashing lights behind us and off we went – I can safely say that I have the honour of being the first person to run the Great North Run. People who saw us must have been wondering what the hell was going on – two motorbikes, a man cycling, and in front of them a man running. Some realised though, and there were shouts of, 'Good on you!'."

However, others were not quite sure. Cherry Alexander, who originates from South Shields, is now a major administrator with UK Athletics. She

has run the Great North Run on two occasions, but worked with Foster and the team on the first 10 races.

She recalls the time Coleby went out measuring. She says: "I remember that one guy rang the police station to say that there was a man pedalling through the central motorway with someone running in front and your guys are doing nothing about it, just following him!"

The route has stayed virtually the same for 24 years. Coleby has not run it since – but he knows every inch of it. His role on race day is to be in the lead car, being first to the finish just as he was in 1981.

Cherry Alexander was another example of the type of person who made the race happen.

She says: "It had a massive impact on me as a youngster. I was 20 and I was working for South Shields Council at the time. I had entered the race, but I had also volunteered to help. Once I had run it, I started handing out medals to the other finishers. Throughout my time working with the people on the race, you could feel their enthusiasm and motivation. Everyone just helped out. Being from South Shields, it was especially exciting knowing that this huge event was taking place on our doorstep. There was so much made about our area because that was where the finish would be."

The start was on the motorway. Each runner would have a start number and they would be penned in together according to their forecast finishing time. It was the responsibility of Dave Roberts, but he had a problem. He would need to put up signs, saying, for example, Numbers 1,000-2,000. He also needed to hang a banner to signal where the race would begin. One of his problems was that he didn't have a ladder to climb up so that he could erect the signs. But he knew a man who did!

Roberts explains: "There was a window cleaner I knew called Ronnie Potts, who was involved with Gateshead Harriers – I had to have someone with a ladder. He was the man."

The late Jimmy Hedley, who died last year, is fondly remembered as the man who coached Steve Cram to his World Championship and world record glory. He had an important part to play in the Great North Run too. He was a joiner by trade and Roberts roped him in to build a podium at the start, from where the officials could watch the race. Roberts explains:

"The start was hung from lampost to lampost and we had marshalling pens with placards up. We had to tie these signs near to the top of the lampost – my dad was the man to tie the banners on – and thanks to another friend, Jimmy, we could climb up to reach things. It was incredible! We had to do things this way because we had no money.

"We did everything on a shoestring. Rediffusion (the television hire company) sponsored the Gateshead International track meeting and they supplied us with a PA system for nothing so that people at the start could hear what was going on. We had help from every quarter imaginable."

The task now was to sift through all the entries, sort out the cheques and solve a problem that everyone who was involved with the first race always remembers. The army had supplied 12 trucks to take the runners' clothes to the finish line, so when the race was over they could change back into tracksuits or whatever dress they felt appropriate.

In their acceptance letter, the organisers had planned to send every runner two copies of their race numbers – one to wear, the other to stick on to a black bag. Those bags would then be sent on different lorries and left in different pens at the finish so the runners would know where to go. On paper it sounds simple, as did the request by the organisers that runners send in a stamped addressed envelope with their cheques. The problem was that some people's reply envelopes were postcard size – not big enough for their race number, let alone a plastic bag.

It all came to a head on a Saturday afternoon when the team gathered at the works canteen of Thorn Gas, who Foster was trying to persuade to sponsor the race.

They had agreed to help out in providing space for his team to go through the painstaking process of transferring every address and every stamp from the envelopes that were too small on to ones that would be big enough for the acceptance kit .

John Caine: "When we all arrived, Brendan was there as we started this arduous task. The first problem was trying to get the air out of the bags to put them into the envelopes. You had to squash them flat. We did not have any computerised system, just 20 or so of us doing this job. Suddenly, after about an hour, a question was asked. Where's Brendan? Where was Brendan! He had gone to York Races as a guest of the sponsors. Okay, they happened to be Thorn, but we were there stuffing envelopes while he was having lunch and a day at the races. We never allowed him to live that one down."

Roberts laughs as he recalls the tale; ironically, 24 years on, he is the man responsible for bringing sponsorship to the race. He can understand Foster's reasoning. He says: "We were so naive, we did not realise how important that meeting with Thorn was. Mind you it didn't seem important at the time! We had 12,000 envelopes in front of us, and there was a human conveyor belt with one person writing out an address, the other replacing a stamp from the envelopes that were too small and then passing it on to the person who put the plastic bags inside. It was a major operation, it was a beautiful day outside and the man in charge was at the races!"

As history recounts, Foster secured Thorn's sponsorship. He says: "I used to run past the offices of Thorn Gas (in the Team Valley in Gateshead) every day. They had heard about the Run, it was taking the North East by storm and we wanted a North East company to be involved in it.

It was good for them. They helped us to keep our head above water."

Acceptance letters had been sent. The start and the finish areas had been worked out. The course had been measured. All the helpers had been primed. The clock was ticking. Wherever you looked, people were running along streets, across parks and through towns and villages. The anticipation of a great day was drawing closer.

My first experiences of 'The Run' were with the generous support of Gateshead Health Authority who arranged for buses to take us to the start and bring us back from the finish. The buses parked on the grass at the seafront by the finish.

Run number two was very wet. We were all soaked through and very tired at the end, and the sight of the buses was very welcome, bringing as they did warm, dry clothes and hot drinks. When everybody had got back to the bus and we were about to set off home, fantasizing about hot baths, the driver revved the engine, released the brake – and we sank deep into the wet ground. Tired, aching bodies then had to get off the bus to push it off the boggy bit!

Catherine (Heather) Oliver
55, Dentist, Isle of Man

64, 65 Making a note of every detail is essential, from timing, to beer to…
It's what makes the day more than just a run.

MATTHEW PINSENT

my part in it...

Recently knighted, four times Olympic Gold medallist and World Championship winning oarsman.

THERE'S no question: as a celebrity runner you get really well looked after at the Great North Run and it's now a regular date in the diary for my wife and I. We actually ran it two weeks before we got married in 2002. I'm always particularly taken with the logistics, how bags are sorted and how the whole event just happens. It's also great to see the huge variety of people running in it, all doing their best – some stopping to ask me the odd question – it's a really friendly occasion.

The disciplines of running and rowing are pretty different – with distance running you need to pound out the miles and weight is not so significant – with rowing you need the power as well.

When I started the race, the whole impression is one of madness with people giving it their all for at least a couple of hours. It's that spirit that most impresses me about the Great North Run.

Chapter 8

WINNERS ALL

AT 11.30pm on Sunday June 28th 1981, Brendan Foster received a knock at the door of his home in Low Fell in Gateshead. It had been one of the longest, most emotional, most gratifying and amazing days of his life, but surely something must be wrong for someone to be wanting him now? He opened his front door to experience the most perfect finish to a spectacular day.

Standing in the cool night air was his friend Phillip Crawley, the Editor of *The Journal*, Newcastle's daily morning newspaper. In his hand, he had the greatest front page Foster had ever seen.

In the early 1980s, newspapers were locked in tradition. There was little colour and rarely would a publication be daring. The next morning, *The Journal* would break all that stuffiness with a newspaper that had a front page devoted to one single picture. It was a shot of thousands upon thousands of runners pouring over the Tyne Bridge. He could not believe it.

If he had any doubts about whether the Great North Run would make an impact on the people of Newcastle, those fears were dismissed by this newspaper, with a photograph depicting the most iconic moment of the event. It had been delivered to his door by the most high profile of paperboys

– the Editor himself – because Crawley wanted Foster to see it before anyone else. Here was confirmation that the Great North Run was more than just a race. It was the news of the day.

Sunday 28th June 1981 began with ludicrously early alarm calls for many people. In fact, some did not sleep at all during the Saturday night because the finishing touches were being made to ensure that everything was in place for the race. Nowadays, the Run has many 'full-time' people involved with its organisation – it is their job. In 1981 it was their hobby, and, because it was so new, there was nothing for Foster and the team to compare it to. If something went wrong, they could not say 'We expected that' because they did not know what to expect.

It was a dull day in the North East. The sun has often made up for it in the years since, but what would have happened if all those people who had promised to help decided to have a lie-in instead? The organisers did not need to have any such worries.

The first crucial point was the shutting of the motorway. Dave Roberts, the man responsible for the start, was there at 3.00 am to oversee the closure so his team could begin building the area

This tale shows the difference in endurance between the average adult and child. I completed the first GNR at the age of 30 and my then four year old son Robbie continually badgered me to be allowed to run with me. Since all he did was run around all day anyway, we finally agreed that he could do the run. For me, the run was the usual 13 miles of sweat and strain, but it appeared to have little or no effect on Robbie, who, with sickening levels of energy, bounced along beside me for the entire 13 miles. The final insult came at 12.5 miles. As I struggled to finish, he excitedly spotted a bouncy castle at the finish line and asked for money to go on it!

We think, at 7, Robbie may have been the youngest official full distance Great North Runner ever to run.

David Gardiner
54, Service Engineer, Lancaster

67 They're off! 12,500 runners get underway at the start of the first Great North Run in 1981.
68, 69 In 1981 when the race took the North East and the running world by storm some areas were a little less well organised, but it was all cleared up and they were back again the next year and every year since. This telling picture of the Tyne Bridge demonstrates the incredible impact the race had.

where 12,500 runners would be converging in a matter of hours. The race had been scheduled to start at 9.30 and Roberts knew that without his team being up to speed, the Great North Run might never happen.

He did not know what he had in store. As he says ruefully, 25 years later, "I thought any trouble we might have would run away from me when the gun sent the runners off." He was about to learn that 12,500 athletes would actually leave behind 25,000 problems for him to deal with. At 4 am in the morning, using street lights to see what they were doing, his team started to prepare. Ronnie Potts, the window cleaner, ladder and all, was busy working away along with Roberts' dad, constructing the start and the pen signs for the runners to line up in.

A big banner was emblazoned across the start, tied to a lampost and a stake in the grass by the verge on the side of the motorway. It was that basic – it was a scene representative of everything happening along the course.

Max Coleby was driving up and down the route, making sure everything was in place. Tables were being set out, the water hydrants were being prepared, thousands of cups were being taken out of their boxes, road closure signs were being prepared, and, as they had promised, Red Cross personnel were taking up their positions... the excitement was growing. Morning was breaking, and as cool dawn broke, the thrill of what was about to happen in a few hours hit the five men.

In a matter of months, since they had first gathered in the Five Bridges, they had put together what would become the greatest athletics event the North East had ever experienced. And now, after all the meetings, all the hard work at the end of their day job, it was finally coming together. John Caine summed it up. "We had started with pieces of a puzzle," he says. "Now on this morning they were all fitting into place and the picture it was producing was there before us."

In front of them were more than 13 miles of road, which in the next few hours would see runners of all shapes and sizes pound their way into history. Proud Geordies, and many others, would later recount to their grandchildren that this was the day when they had run in the same race as Steve Cram, Brendan Foster and other stars from the world of athletics.

By eleven o'clock, the runners were starting to arrive and the operation was in full flow. The army had provided 12 trucks where the runners would place the black bags full of clothes that they would pick up at the finish.

It seemed a logical plan. Truck A, for athletes between numbers 1-1,000. Stick your bag in there and when you reach the finish line, pen 1-1,000 will have your bags. On paper, it sounded wonderful, but it did not quite work out that way.

Caine made his way to the start as the runners began arriving. They had accepted 12,500 entries but there was no way of knowing how many would actually make the start. It had all been put together through the mailing to the BBC, and while there was a telephone helpline for people who had lost numbers or needed some advice, there was no actual information as to how many would be there on the day.

Foster was flabbergasted. He recalls: "We knew we had 12,500 entries – but when we arrived at the start we did not know what that was going to look like.

"The regular guys who used to run in local road races were there and they could not believe it. People were arriving from everywhere. There were so many of them. People were just jumping up and down at the start to try and look back down the road. They could not believe the scene."

Unlike today, when the elite part of the race is a major event, this opening Great North Run was very much a local affair. But that was elite enough. Mike McLeod, Jim Alder, Steve Cram and of course Foster, all running together, were enough to whet the appetite. Never mind the footballing hero of the North East taking part too.

Foster had persuaded Kevin Keegan, the Southampton and England captain to run. With a wonderful touch of unity, he wore a specially-made shirt that had the black and white stripes of Newcastle down one half and the red and white of arch rivals Sunderland on the other. Talk about making friends and influencing people. Keegan did it with this magical touch.

The race was started by the firing of a 25lb field gun, which had been supplied by the Royal Artillery from their base in Catterick, 80 miles away. Naturally, it made 'one hell of a boom' as Caine puts it, so it meant the race director making an important visit...to the nearby Royal Victoria Infirmary Hospital.

He says: "They had a maternity wing and we had to advise them of the precise time that the cannon was going off because we didn't want to cause any premature births! Nowadays, regulations mean you cannot use such a gun. But then it was different and we needed something that loud so the runners back along the motorway could hear it."

While the gun was operated by soldiers, starting the race became one of the honours of the day

– and the man selected for the inaugural event was a man who had done so much to promote it. There could no better choice than the BBC's Mike Neville to send the runners on their way. It is an experience he has never forgotten.

He says: "I sat in the middle of this damn great cannon, the saddle went back and: Wow! When you look at the television replays of the start, when the gun goes off, all you can see is me mouthing 'Jesus Christ'."

With that, the runners in the first Great North Run were on their way, taking the opening steps on the path that has taken the event into history as the world's biggest half-marathon. It was a sight to behold, an astonishing mass of people bounding along.

Neville continues: "I had tears streaming down my face as all these runners came by and next to me, there were all these big butch soldiers with tears too. It was astonishing. The spectators were as excited as the runners."

Coleby and Roberts had climbed on to one of the bridges across the motorway and looked down on the amazing scenes below them. "It was something else," says Coleby. "But I don't think John Trainor, who was responsible for the finish, knew what was going to hit him!"

What was worse is that they could not tell him. They did not have any form of communication;

1984

Three events dominated 1984: there was the bitter year-long Miner's Strike, called to protest against the closure of many of Britain's ailing coal pits; in October, the IRA planted a bomb which tore apart the Brighton Grand Hotel where members of the Cabinet were staying for the Conservative party conference, causing two deaths and some serious injuries; and a relentless and terrible famine in Ethiopia. TV news reports alerted the world to the humanitarian crisis in the Horn of Africa and British response was swift if unorthodox. Pop singers Bob Geldof and Midge Ure formed the star-studded group Band Aid and their single 'Do They Know It's Christmas' raised £8 million to help the starving. Besides hunger, war and drought, the world had to come to terms with a new and virulent disease when, in April, scientists announced the discovery of the HIV virus that caused AIDS. But if Orwell's vision of a bleak future for humanity seemed to be coming true in 1984, there were lighter moments. The first episode of the satire show Spitting Image was broadcast and essential fashion items included baggy white T-shirts emblazoned with the words Frankie Says...Relax, (inspired by the number one single from Frankie Goes to Hollywood that was banned by Radio One) and the Filofax.

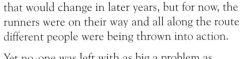

70, 71 *Steve Cram (top left) and Brendan Foster (top right) were star names of the day as was the starter of the race, the BBC's Mike Neville. Disabled athletes who are now so pivotal to the race's prowess were also a welcome sight.*

that would change in later years, but for now, the runners were on their way and all along the route different people were being thrown into action.

Yet no-one was left with as big a problem as Roberts, the man who had been put in charge of the start and had famously said the problems would be running away from him. He could not have been more wrong.

The organisers were aware that athletes could not be expected to wait for long periods before the race wearing only their singlets and shorts because of potential bad weather, so they had advised

them to arrive in, if possible, old clothes that they could take off and literally throw away when the race began. The majority of the 12,500 runners did just that.

Roberts explains: "We had this sea of people, the gun went off and I took a deep breath when they all disappeared because I thought my job had been done. Then I looked back down the road and it was like a battleground. The motorway was littered with 12,500 people's gear – from old jumpers to trousers.

"They had done what we had asked them to. They had worn old clothes and had ditched them when the race began – and we were left to clear up. My group of family and friends were there and I thought 'What am I going to do?' The road had to open soon. I had lots of help from rugby clubs and friends of friends but as soon as the race started, they went, so those of us left had to clear up the mess. We put the clothes into piles and the lorries that were still there picked it up. It was unbelievable."

By now, the race was in full swing. The atmosphere at the front was extraordinary and race leader Mike McLeod decided that he was going to enjoy every second. He did not have anything to prove by leading – he was a big enough name in British athletics – but he wanted to be at the forefront of a race being run in his home town in front of his people.

"When the first Great North Run began, none of us knew what was in store," says McLeod, who lives six miles from the start in Wideopen. "All we knew was that there was a half–marathon, going from point A to B, through three boroughs.

"I had taken a car down to the finish early that morning so I would have no problem coming home afterwards. Even then there were people on the side of the road, waiting for the race to start. People wanted to make sure that they had the best vantage points and the crowds on the route were absolutely tremendous. There was so much noise, that you had to stay in the middle of the course, because if you were on one side, their noise sent you back across. It was extraordinary."

Caine agrees. He says: "In that first year, the crowd was colossal – there was the uniqueness and novelty value of the first event."

McLeod, then 28, went straight to the front, and of his many memories of the occasion, nothing beats what he saw when he made his way across the Tyne Bridge, in the second mile of the race. He says: "On another of the bridges nearby, a train had stopped. The drivers had climbed out and they were just watching the event. I don't know if they were on their way to London, but wherever they were going, the passengers can't have been too happy."

The organisers had invited one foreign international, Oyvind Dahl, of Norway. But there was no stopping McLeod. He stamped his authority on the race straight away. The first mile is downhill, and he ran it in 4:15 – a world record pace – and the quickest that McLeod has ever run in a road race. He could see the time on the clock on the lead car in front of him. It was an old white Jaguar coupé with a black roof, with Coleby on board.

Someone suggested that the clock was wrong because of the time McLeod was running. "I remember Max shouting back 'The clock's not wrong. It is him. He's running that quickly'," recalls McLeod.

He was savouring this remarkable experience. He was stretching his lead and while the mass of runners were making their way behind him, it was clear there was going to be only one winner – and a fitting one too, a North East hero.

Behind him, though, there were individual cameos and stories unfolding with every mile – and at the BBC, a frantic day of work. They had a programme scheduled for 5.30pm to review the race. For John Bird, the Editor of *Look North*, who had played such a key part in the race's success, it was one of the most memorable days of his working life.

Bird says: "We were still working on film. The nightmare came when we had to process and edit it and get it ready for the programme that was going out a few hours later.

"We had wheeled a studio camera out with all its cabling onto a footbridge that looked up to the start. That was an emotional moment because everyone remembers the runners coming across the Tyne Bridge. Suddenly, there was this mass of people going over the Bridge, the cry went up 'Oggy, Oggy, Oggy'.

"You can ask people 'Where were you when Kennedy was assassinated?' They will know, and in the North East they will tell you where they were when the first Great North Run took place."

But Bird could not rest. It was a time before satellites and state-of-the-art feeds. It was going to take some effort to get this programme on air – and what was worse, one of its stars, Foster, was somewhere amidst the throng of 12,500 people.

Although Foster had retired from the track the previous summer and was now a part of the BBC commentary team, the event was not being shown live that first year and there was little doubt that he had to run in it. He was 34, but a young runner, Steve Cram, was no respecter of seniority. The pair started the race together – but it did not stay that way.

Foster says: "Crammy had run in the 1980 Olympics in Moscow in the 1,500m against Seb

In 2002 a leukaemia victim affectionately nicknamed Bison inspired 50 twenty-something friends to run the BUPA Great North Run and raise an astonishing £150,000 for Leukaemia Research.

Ian Lane, 26, died of acute myeloid leukaemia in September 2001 and his university friends decided to take up the half-marathon challenge as a tribute to him. Ian was known as 'Bison' because of his powerful, 6ft 4in build. He was a skilled track-and-field athlete and once accidentally broke a vaulting pole because he attacked it with such energy.

One of the team, Samantha Day, commented on her friend "It's horribly ironic that Ian was always the healthiest of us all, always urging us to get fit. He was the last person you'd think would get so sick. At the finishing line, there were 50 very relieved people thinking only of Ian and how funny he would have thought it that his crisp-munching, fag-smoking, beer-swilling, lazy bunch of mates had achieved something so brilliant."

Since the run in 2002 many members from Team Bison have gone on to run further events from the Great Run series, having fun, remembering their friend and raising further much needed funds for Leukaemia Research.

Fiona Watson
Sporting Events Co-ordinator, Leukaemia Research

72, 73 *The scale of the Great North Run is what sets it apart. When the masses finish and cross the Tyne Bridge it's as if an army is on the move.*

Coe and Steve Ovett. I had decided to run it because it was the first.

"I set off and forgot all about him. We got to eight or nine miles and I was running on memory, rather than on fitness, and Crammy came alongside me. He was going well – and he was saying 'Isn't this great, wonderful,' and I just could not reply. I was knackered. I told him to 'Bugger off!'

"He ran away and for the last four miles, he was about 100 yards ahead of me, looking over his shoulder and laughing. He was running strongly, but he was not trying to win it."

Cram recounts his version: "In those days, the field was not as big as it is now, and at the front, the club standard was high. Brendan was not that far behind and the plan was that we were going to run together. It never happened.

"I lost him very quickly because he went off a lot harder than he said he was going to. I settled into a pace, I was pretty fit and I started reeling people in, and lo and behold, I caught Brendan at about the 10-mile mark. I was going to run in with him then. He was starting to suffer and he told me simply to 'Bugger off!'."

Foster, naturally, was gaining more support from the crowd and fellow runners than anyone else. He explains: "People were cheering but I was gone. I could not respond. I was trying to take in the whole occasion but I was too knackered. I was 100 yards behind Crammy, 100 yards ahead of the next bloke. But you couldn't absorb the scale of it until you saw the whole thing on television."

McLeod, who won again the next year and finished second on two more occasions, was an ideal winner. He was from the North East, his career was blooming and from the outset it gave the race athletic excellence.

He triumphed in 1:03:23, from Dahl in 1:04:34 with Britain's Mike Kearns third in 1:04:39. The first woman home was Royal Air Force member Karen Goldhawk from South Shields Harriers, in 1:17:36. Second home was Margaret Lockley, in 1:20:36 with Mary Chambers third in 1:26:24.

Meantime, the clock was ticking down at BBC HQ as the thousands of runners poured across the finish line. Another local hero, Kevin Keegan, also made it – but as he crossed the finish, the blisters on his feet were so bad that he had to be carried to the medical tent.

Coleby had to overcome even more problems at the finish on the South Shields road. The intention had been to have traffic going south towards Sunderland while the race took place on the other side of the carriageway.

He explains: "Before Christmas, I had gone to Otterburn Army camp. I saw the junior regiment leader and convinced the army to provide me with enough soldiers to stand at 10 metre intervals along the course to keep all the runners on the correct side of the road, separated from the cars. On the day it lasted about ten minutes before the roads were swamped. It caused complete chaos with the traffic because nothing could go south."

It was not the only place where things were not exactly going to plan.

Beyond the finish line, as the runners received their medal and T-shirt, they were directed to various pens to collect their clothes so that they could change. Logically, everything made sense... black bags with a runner's number on. The only problem was that the trucks dropping off the black bags did just that – dropped them off anywhere and everywhere. Picture the scene of 12,500 black bags all together.

It was like looking for a needle in a stack of needles and the general view taken was that people actually gave up looking into this sea of black – and went home in their running kits!

Meanwhile at the finish line, people were collapsing with exhaustion, others were just finishing, but for some, there was unexpected inspiration. Steve Donaldson, a runner from Gateshead who had been lured into the event by the publicity, was struggling to make it to the finish. He had a mile to go and he was not sure he was going to make it. He says: "There was no way I wanted to stop, having gone this far, and then suddenly I saw this little old lady, living in one of the houses near the finish. She had come out to cheer us all on and had put the music from *Chariots of Fire* on. It was blaring out from her house – I did not need anything more to help me."

Coleby, despite various plans not going as they had been intended to, also remembers the scene clearly: "I was standing with a loudspeaker shouting to runners to slow down at the finish – but they were hyper at completing the race, and we were delighted too. People were shaking our hands and thanking us – the Great North Run had worked."

The first man across the line, Mike McLeod, remains the only athlete from the North East to win the race. McLeod, who progressed to win Olympic 10,000m silver in Los Angeles in 1984, says: "The first Great North Run stands out for me. If it had been anywhere else in the country, it would not have been the same.

"Today, people come from around the world and take holidays around the race to run in it. You are now talking about a world-class race. It is not an

1985

This was the year Vodafone launched the first cellular phone service in the UK, closely followed by rivals Cellnet who were backed by the newly privatised British Telecom. However, football fans will remember 1985 for very different reasons as 1985 was the year of not one but two appalling tragedies. On May 11th, the 77-year-old wooden stand at Bradford City's Valley Parade ground burned to ashes and 56 spectators died. Two weeks later, the European Cup Final, held in Brussels, also turned to disaster when crowd trouble between rival Liverpool and Juventus supporters caused part of the Heysel Stadium's terracing to collapse. Yet for all this bad news, 1985 was not entirely devoid of hope. In July the world witnessed just what could be achieved with a little co-operation thanks to the extraordinary Live Aid event staged simultaneously in London and Philadelphia. The concert, inspired by the success of Band Aid, and headlined by David Bowie, Mick Jagger, Dire Straits and Queen, raised a staggering £40 million for African famine relief.

easy course, and it can be fast if you get a tail wind from west to east, but you have to be fit and you have to turn those legs over."

After starting the run, Mike Neville had taken a boat along the Tyne to make it to the finish. He missed McLeod's triumph, but the tears were back.

He explains: "When the last runners passed me at the start, a car whisked Brendan's wife and I to the quayside where a large police launch was waiting for us. We sped down the Tyne where another car was waiting for us – and by the time we got there, Mike McLeod had already finished.

"But then the wheelchair finishers came through. The emotion was amazing. It was just like the start had been. There were three burly policeman standing with me, we had been talking and then they too had tears running down their faces. A colleague of mine had come to see it, he was standing crying with joy – and suddenly I realised, so was I."

There would have been tears of a different kind had his other job not gone to plan.

Foster and Neville were taken by helicopter back into Newcastle to present the programme for the BBC. It was 5.28 with two minutes to go. The programme had not been finished. It was 5.29. Still no film was there. Ten seconds. Nine, eight, seven, six, five, four, three, two and – the tape entered the machine – one. On air!

Bird says: "We literally started the programme as they counted it down. We had just finished the film and got it into the machine. We pressed the button – and out it went.

"After that, once it became so popular, London studios sent up their own teams. But on that first year, we were making and mending as we went along. On that first run it was a wet day, and the helicopter we were filming from recorded little more than the start before it had to go back to the airport because of the conditions.

"We had a camera at the start, and on the route, but it was all film. All the journalists had sequences to do – it was a huge job and we had to make sure these sequences were put together. The only two outside broadcast cameras were at the start and a smaller one was on the Tyne Bridge. We saw it as a challenge. It was the biggest operation of its time."

Neville recalls the events around him: "The entire BBC North East team turned out. People who were on days off came in. We said we would never hit 5.30 for the half hour show.

"Scripts were coming in while we were on air – and then I would link to a piece of film. It worked

74, 75 Today the Race is acknowledged as the world's largest half-marathon. Back on June 29 1981 The Journal signalled the beginning of an illustrious start to an extraordinary event.

and at the end, Brendan and I just looked at each other and hugged. There had been no mistakes, everything went perfectly, with no rehearsals."

That night, all the runners around Newcastle were wearing their T-Shirts and had a medal around their neck. They were going out for a drink wearing their T-shirt. "It might not be cool to do it now but then it was a real badge of honour," says Caine.

It had been some day. People who had never run before had completed a half-marathon – and the organisers knew that the many charities people had run for were going to gain immensely. Bird provides one of the best stories. "A man was so determined to do it," he says. "That he completed the whole course on crutches."

People had dressed up, but the craze which has now developed in the race for odd costumes had not yet caught on. The sight of thousands just running was enough to capture everyone's imagination.

As it had across the city that night at the headquarters of *The Journal* where Phillip Crawley, the Editor, went into his office having run the race. It led to a classic decision.

He says: "I had run in the race, and I had a sense of excitement of what type of occasion it had been and how the crowds had turned out. The person who was designing the front page had the picture and he was using it in the usual way. I said 'No, no, we have to go big'. He asked 'How big?'

"We played around with it for a while and eventually said let's go for broke. The picture was full page, top to bottom. The sales the following day proved us right. People had seen it on the television or taken part the previous day and they wanted a souvenir. We then did a poster of that famous picture. That sold very well, it was the first time anyone had seen the whole of the Tyne Bridge covered with this mass of humanity."

The paper produced an four-page special inside, a copy of which Crawley had tucked under his arm when he arrived at Foster's house that night.

Inside, Foster and his family had been reflecting on the Run. But did they really know how big the story was? He answered his door and saw the paper.

Foster sums it up: "You could not play in the FA Cup Final and you could not play in The Open Golf Championship. But you could run the Great North Run; it was an achievable dream. People had lived that dream.

"When I saw that paper, I realised what we had done – but I also thought it was just the beginning."

RUNNING TO TIME

76, 77 Since 1981 the iconic Tyne Bridge has found a younger, glorious brother – the Millennium Bridge. It's the landmark that joins Newcastle with Gateshead's Quay and a symbol of regeneration. It's also part of the route for the Mile Races and Junior Great North Run which take place on the Saturday of the Great North Run weekend. Here, the Red Arrows, another favourite part of the weekend mirror the Bridge's architectural beauty to spectacular effect.

John Williamson

1981

SUCH was the success of the inaugural Great North Run, there was no question but it would become a permanent fixture, although in what form Brendan Foster did not know and could not have imagined. Within hours of the first race finishing, the enthusiasm for another Great North Run was overwhelming.

Twenty-four years on, and much has changed. As the organisers of the event prepare for the celebrations of this year's Run, they already know the date of the race in 2006 and beyond. It was anything but the case in 1981. Now, it is a professional organisation called Nova International, where Foster is the chairman and four of the original quintet who started the event are still involved.

In 1999, the BUPA Great North Run had become so high profile that BBC Television gave it its own slot on a Sunday morning. Nowadays, four hours are shown live with a recorded highlights programme in the evening – and it is a measure of the direction the race has gone in that as many hours are devoted to the fun and charity runners as to the elite at the sharp end of the proceedings.

Of course, without the race being able to attract the likes of Britain's marathon world record holder, Paula Radcliffe, the Run would not have the profile it does. But equally, without the majority of the 48,000 runners behind those elite runners, it would be just another race for the likes of Radcliffe.

The Great North Run has reached the age of 25 having encompassed every emotion: joy, sadness, worry, delight, expectation, enlightenment, hope, despair. There is also an acceptance that time moves on and if you don't change with it, like a tiring runner you will be left behind.

But during those past 24 races, a unique, official 'club' has been formed, comprising the runners who have taken part in every race. At the end of last year's Great North Run, there were 146 still holding that proud record. They have all been invited back again – no longer needing to apply for an official entry.

Anne Wilson, 58, is a headmistress from Whitley Bay. She is one of the 146 and she is an extraordinary character. Along with her husband Ernie, they run each year wearing different costumes as they make their way from Newcastle to South Shields carrying buckets to raise money for charity.

78, 79 The mass ranks cross the Bridge. Meanwhile at the finish Kevin Keegan (bottom right) sprints for glory.

She had never run any distance before seeing Mike Neville and Foster announce the race on BBC *Look North* in the spring of 1981. But to her, it is more than just a run. "If there is one thing that every Geordie should do before they die, it is to take part in the Great North Run," she says, "There is nothing like it. The camaraderie, the atmosphere, the experience. It is amazing."

But while the emotion is tangible the training is a little less formal. Three weeks before the run, she and her husband (who has run 22) go out for long Sunday walks, the only 'training' they need to be ready. As she says: "Times do not matter. We are there for the reason of just wanting to be in the Great North Run. Our lives would not be the same without it."

How is it that this half-marathon course has had such an effect on people?

With some clever management and a great deal of tender loving care, the Great North Run has become just what Foster wanted it to be – a race of the people, packed with fun and determination and the odd world record. In the heart of the race, friendships are made and personal stories are created, celebrities mix with Joe Jogger and loved ones are remembered by the achievements of those running in their memory. The race has seen more than its share of heroes and, occasionally, villains, but in its 25th year it has never been in better shape.

Mark Shearman

photographer: John Caine
John Caine

Evening Chronicle and Journal Ltd

80-83 Warming down and relaxation. Everybody has their own preferences, but some competitors take longer than others to finish. Richard Redhead (page 80) completes the course on crutches in 1982, just enjoying a weekend walk.

1982

A year on from the rip-roaring triumph of the first came the second Run, on June 27th – and with it another 7,500 people were added to the start line.

It proved to be even more astonishing than the first year. On March 14, 1982, when the official announcement was made, more than 11,000 entry forms were accepted at the offices of BBC North. In the end, 50,000 people wanted to run – and 30,000 had to be turned away. Says Brendan Foster: "The Great North Run is a half-marathon and that is one of the secrets of its success. Keeping it down to 13.1 miles makes it easier for people; to the fun runner it is more appealing."

Now, one year on, lessons had been learned. Such was the frenzy at the finish in 1981, when some people went home without collecting their kit because they simply could not find it, that the organisers put this problem at the top of their list. By 1982, with an even larger field, they decided to have a series of buses which the runners would put their belongings on to before the race. The buses would then drive down the course, and be in place at the finish where the runners would be able to collect their clothes. It was simple and it worked, and still does.

By this second year, there was also a family reunion section at the finish, and four finishing lines side by side, to accommodate the growing number of runners. There was also a new request to the runners: "Please resist the temptation to stop or collapse once you have crossed the line."

By the time the race was started – again by Mike Neville – the status of the event had grown to a level where it was making news long before the cannon was fired.

Hobbling home, Richard Redhead, 66, from Chester-Le-Street, completed the run on crutches. He had sustained a leg injury in training, but he was determined nothing would stop him taking part. "I was told before the start that the crowd would keep me going and by God they did," he said after the race. "I was proud to compete."

There were 17,500 finishers. Enough to see the run enter the Guinness Book of World Records as the largest road race in Europe.

1983

'GREAT NORTH RUN IN DOUBT' the headline screamed. Suddenly there was a fear that with the ink not even dry on the pages of the Guinness Book of World Records, the race might not have a future. Beneath the words was a picture of Brendan Foster. It was 40 days since the Run and four of the Five Bridges men were working for Nike, the sportswear company. Foster was the Director of the local branch of the company; John Caine, Dave Roberts and John Trainor all now worked together in offices in Durham.

Through Nike, they helped to organize the race. But now there was a suggestion that Nike were about to move to London or the Midlands and as Foster said at the time: "With the best will in the world, we could not organise the Great North Run from a distance. If we moved as a company, it would be beyond us."

Fortunately it never came to that, as Nike moved to Washington in County Durham and the future of the Great North Run was safe, especially when Thorn EMI Heating Limited agreed to sponsor the race for the next three years. It had become an instant triumph. Gordon Sargent, the Sales Director of the company, sums it up: "The Great North Run is one of the best examples of company sponsorship because it has everything we ask of it and it benefits us on a large scale, not merely focusing on a minority interest." There was then further good news when the police allowed the field to be increased to 21,500.

In 1983, Kevin Keegan was back – but he became the figure at the centre of an extraordinary controversy. A few days before the race, Foster received a call from a member of the Amateur Athletic Association, the sport's national governing body, telling him that his race was illegal.

Nowadays, featuring paid professional competitors is the lifeblood of an athletics event. The elite field is paid hundreds of thousands of pounds to make the Great North Run and numerous other races the international attractions they have become. In 1983, true amateurism was slowly disappearing but the traditionalists wanted to hold on. The Great North Run became a prime target.

The AAA kicked up a fuss because they had learnt that Kevin Keegan, the England football captain, had agreed to run the race again. In their code book this made it illegal for the top amateur runners, such as the UK's Mike McLeod, to be in the same race, because they were breaking the 'contamination' rule. This stated that professional sportsmen could not compete in amateur events and if they did, amateur athletes would face a ban.

Keegan was the professional in question. It didn't

Bryn Lennon/Getty Images

matter that it was in football, not athletics – and despite the fact that he had run unchallenged in the first race.

Foster remains baffled to this day about what then followed. He says: "I told them if they were going to ban anyone, they could start with me. There was no way I was telling 20,000 people that the race was off, so I told the AAA that they could come down to the start, we would give them a megaphone and a box to stand on and they could tell those 20,000 people the race was off."

It was not only Keegan. Fellow footballer Chris Waddle was also running, but there was a principle at stake and Foster was in no mood to give in.

At the time, the promotions officer of the AAA was Andy Norman. Foster knew him well. Norman intervened and the row was prevented in a way that made the whole debacle seem even more ludicrous.

Foster recalls: "He came up with a brilliant idea of having the Great North Run and the Great North Fun Run. No one knew, the runners themselves had no idea. But what we did was paint a white line across the road. In front of it stood the international athletes, and behind the line stood another 19,000 or so people – including Keegan and Waddle – as the professionals."

The AAA were happy. It remained one run in everyone's eyes, except to those who had made the fuss. What made the bid to stop the race seem all the more ludicrous was that Keegan himself did not actually run the race for the second time. He was now a player with Newcastle United and, for charity, he was pushing muscular dystrophy sufferer Peter May. But a wheel fell off the chair.

"I don't know how it happened, but suddenly we had broken down," said Keegan. Peter said: "I thought the race was over when the wheel came off, but there were dozens of people who rushed forward to help and we were soon on our way again."

Not everyone could say the same. Michael Thompson, of Stockton-on-Tees, who has run all 24, did not know what had happened when Keegan ran into him with the wheelchair.

Thompson was sent flying. Keegan helped him up and across to a first-aider. Thompson recalls the incident: "He ran into me and I fell to the floor. Whilst the medic was examining my injuries I asked him if he knew the culprit as he had called him by his first name, Kevin. To which the reply was; 'Sure, did you not recognise Kevin Keegan?' Not being a football fan I hadn't the faintest idea who he was."

But one overriding factor stood out in 1983.

The weather was the hottest in the run's history, and in temperatures around 75 degrees, the race suffered a death. Over 2,000 runners received aid from medical staff and at times people were fighting over water at drinking stations – some taking three cups when there was only enough for one each.

In summary, this run showed a few human failings, but even the warmest temperatures could not prevent another great success.

1984

THE first 'casualty' of the Great North Run in this year was Brendan Foster; he had competed in previous races but a calf injury suffered while training meant he would have to watch this one from the sidelines. However, he was unable to watch it from the BBC Commentary box because the corporation did not show the event live. With European elections as well as other sporting events all requiring outside broadcasting equipment, there was just not enough at BBC Newcastle to go round.

This meant that even more people came out onto the streets of the North East to watch the event – spectator numbers growing towards an estimated 200,000. The noise was immense, and this time, there were more than enough drinks to go around – the organisers now were allowed a field of 25,000.

Along with the increasing numbers, one other aspect of the race that was growing each time was the amount of money being raised for charity. At least a million pounds every race and, in conjunction with the London Marathon, the two events were the biggest fund-raising days of the year.

It's nice to be recognised for the achievement of having completed all 24 runs. Looking back over the years to my first training session, I was reasonably fit, being a local footballer, and thought: 'Running 13.1 miles is easy', but after a 10 mile run I couldn't walk for a week. I managed the Great North Run in 1:47, no bother, and I was hooked. Numerous fun-runs followed and attracted family members and I made lots of new friends'.

One year, it was so hot I decided to smother vaseline all over my body. At the end of the race I ran straight into the sea, cooked! I looked like a lobster and agony followed.

In 1993 I had a cartilage operation. 'No run for you,' the doctor said. However, after some training, starting with 10 minutes jogging on the spot, I completed the run in over 3 hours! In 2001 I twisted an ankle playing 5-a-side four days before the race. I strapped it up, took some painkillers and somehow came home in little over two hours.

In the days of the lottery for numbers I was devastated not to get in one year but luckily got a number from a friend. In 2002 my place was again in danger when I found out from a friend that the run was full. All had applied on-line. Devastated I phoned around, but to no avail. Then a glimmer of hope arrived... 1000 places available as a lottery in the Journal. After weeks of letterbox watching my acceptance came through.

One year my Mam said, 'If you lot can do it, so can I.' She entered at 70 years' old and with no training. Her claim to fame was that she finished last, but smiling.

I often stop to talk to spectators who watch year after year and find out sadly who has died. One year I was informed of a man who had passed on. What a shock when I later spoke to his 'ghost', as large as life!

In 2003 we ran for the Baldy Bros. from Metro Radio. At the start line a bucket was thrust into my hand. Immediately, copper coins were thrown in, some loose, some in prepared £1 bags. I struggled after halfway with aches and pains all over my body!

Ron Snaith
Cramlington

84, 85 *Flower Power and heavenly Fathers. It takes all sorts. Newly weds Kevin and Katherine Denton are surely blessed.*

Picture Loan: Keith And Katherine Denton

As with London, people would dress up to run – but on Sunday June 17, a young couple wearing bride and groom clothes were doing it for real.

Twenty-four hours earlier, Keith and Katherine Denton had been married. But the Run was such a part of their life that it had be included in some way.

"We must have been crackers," says Katherine. "We booked the wedding and for some reason did not even think it would clash with the race. When we found out it was going to, we didn't have a choice. We were not going to miss it!"

Keith, now 50, of Low Fell, Gateshead, had run the first race in 1981 along with Katherine's father, Jim Hart. "I watched that one and thought 'I would like to do that'," says Katherine. Since then, she has run in 22, and her husband and father are part of The 146 Club.

Katherine, 47, tells us more: "The media caught onto it and we were featured in the newspapers and on television." She adds: 'We stayed in the Post House Hotel in Washington on our wedding night and by 7.30 the next morning we were up

having breakfast. We did not get much sleep. We were running on adrenaline and I was absolutely knackered, but, as one of my bridesmaids said, we had to go through with it. We completed the Great North Run and on the Monday morning we drove down to the South of France and Spain for our honeymoon."

1985

WHEN Brendan Foster and his team were compiling the start lists for the 1985 race, one name would not have been put forward. Steve Kenyon had been among the top distance runners in the country, but as far as everyone knew he had retired the previous year.

This makes the fact that this year he became the last British man to win the Great North Run both ironic and staggering. In the 20 years since he triumphed, the event has become the domain of the African runners, a runner from that continent being triumphant on 13 occasions.

Some top British men, from Steve Jones, the former marathon world record holder, to Paul Evans, and then Andy Coleman in 2000, have finished second. But in the last four years no runner from the UK has been in the top three of the men's event. In Britain, the middle-distance era of Sebastian Coe, Steve Ovett, Steve Cram and Peter Elliott remains at a standard that has not been matched in recent times.

Thankfully, for the women runners things have been different. Paula Radcliffe's rise has been phenomenal, and that of Kelly Holmes, especially at Athens 2004, has been sensational.

At 53, Steve Kenyon now works in a sportswear shop in Bolton, his home town, and never would have imagined in 1985 that twenty years on he would still remain the last triumphant Briton. In fact, it was a British 1-2-3 back then when Kenyon beat Mike McLeod, the winner in 1981 and 1982, and Bernie Ford.

He can't think why things have developed this way. "When I was competing, you could roll off names such as Brendan Foster, Dave Bedford, Bernie Ford, Dave Black, Mike McLeod, Nick Rose – the list goes on and on.

"In 1980 I was a member of the England team that won the World Cross-Country Championships in Paris. It is now twenty-five years since that happened. Maybe the British hunger and desire is not there."

Every year since, in a similar way to the Great North Run, the World Team Title has been won by either Ethiopia or Kenya.

In 1985, Kenyon had come out of a dreadful previous year. He announced his retirement because he had become so frustrated with injuries. After an operation, he returned to some light training which he built up and then he decided to enter the Great North Run.

86, 87 *The early birds catch the best view while the smiling North East spectators are relished by all the runners.*

"I did not even receive an official invite which would have included my accommodation," he says. "I was coached by Gordon Surtees. I stayed with another of his athletes in Stockton and we made our way to Newcastle on the morning of the race.

"I went into it with quite an open mind, not knowing what to expect. It was the first time that I had run it."

The North East had been a good area for Kenyon because he had previously won the AAA Marathon in 1982 which started and finished at the Gateshead International Stadium and included parts of the Great North Run course.

He progressed to the European Championships that year which were staged in Athens. He continues: "I had a bad run on the same course that Paula Radcliffe ran in 2004 and I dropped out as well. That was when I decided to knock marathons on the head and to concentrate on shorter stuff."

By 1985, having failed to make the Olympic team in Los Angeles the previous year, Kenyon rediscovered his enthusiasm. "It all seemed to fit into place. There was a group of us including Mike McLeod, Bernie Ford, and Alistair Hutton. We reached seven miles, I was feeling fresh and I started to open up a small gap.

"I have watched the video from the live recording and Brendan in the commentary says 'Steve is making an early bid for victory.' But slowly, as we reached 10-11 miles, his tone changed. I started to feel the lack of training and preparation when I was running on the coast road and my pace did drop there. But I stayed in front."

He became one of the race's most unexpected winners when he triumphed in 1:02:44. A year later, he returned to finish third, behind fellow Briton Steve Jones in a run won by Mike Musyoki, of Kenya. It was the start of a familiar story.

SIR JIMMY SAVILE OBE KCSG

my part in it...

Former DJ and television personality and 'peerless' fundraiser for charity.

(Sir Jimmy has taken part in 23 Great North Runs and 217 marathons in total)

If you live long enough you can be amazed at the twists and turns in life's journey. For me, the Great North Run is just one of those twists and turns.

In 1936, when I was 10, an auntie lived just off Prince Edward Road. Leaving her house at about 8 am I would walk two miles to the magical Marsden Beach. With not a penny in my pocket, it seemed the entire world was skint. With no food or drink, I would spend all day on the beach and under Marsden Rock, walking back at about 5 pm, totally happy.

From 1936, turn the clock forward to 1981.

Once again I am on Prince Edward Road but this time with thousands of friends in the Great North Run. A Rolls Royce car is waiting for me at the finish along with three TV crews and several newspapers. All quite amazing for the twists and turns along the road of life.

But running down Prince Edward Road I am once again 10 years old, no money and still full of happiness. What a strange, wonderful world it is for some of us.

88, 89 Runner and television personality Sir Jimmy Savile has run for fun for many a year. He's one of the great characters of the race but there are many, many more to meet of all shapes and sizes and all backgrounds.

John Williamson

Katy Melling

John Williamson

John Williamson

Before the first Great North Run a number of players from the Acklam Rugby Club were sitting in the local Squash Club Bar discussing the dramatic events of the first London marathon. After a few more beers about six of us decided to enter the GNR.

No real problem, we thought, and we duly arranged a coach to take us to the start. As we were pinning our numbers on, just before alighting, we noticed Peter Welsh pinning on his number which I think was about number 60.

'How the hell did you get such a low number?' we asked. All our numbers consisted of five digits or more.

It turns out that when filling the form in for his estimated time he had approximated a run that we used for rugby training and multiplied the time up to come to 1 hour, not realising this was better than the world record. However having set off in his rugby shorts and plimsolls (yes, plimsolls!) he managed to complete the run in a very respectable time of 1 hour 20 minutes and on the starting line got Kevin Keegan to sign his white rugby shorts.

Ray Kelly
Retired Engineer, Middlesbrough

90, 91 Top 90 – The Gurkhas complete the course in step, showing impressive training and fitness. Others need a little help but are still winners

British Red Cross First Aid Post

was and he was about to take it to the race's lost property section. Everyone stopped to clap as the gorilla made it home. The man inside the suit crossed the line, saw Coleby, saw the wallet and said, "Thanks mate. I really appreciate you looking after it for me!"

There was also the story of a man who was so worn out by the time he reached the start – having already run for 20 minutes just to get there because of the mass of people in front of him – that he gave up after two metres, sat down and said: "Enough is enough!"

It was through stories such as these, and many, many more beside, that the spirit of the Great North Run grew – and each year more and more spectators helped the runners in any way they could.

Not that every bit of 'help' was always wanted. But moments of idiocy were more than counterbalanced by the brilliance of the charity runners – with the funds raised increasing by the million with each year of the race. Everyone always looked for different ways to bring in as much cash as they could, and in 1986 twenty soldiers from the King Edward VII's Own Gurkhas completed the race – in step all the way – for Leukaemia Research.

1986

AS course director, Max Coleby watches the races from the lead car. But perhaps his most extraordinary story came when the race was over.

The people at the start were slowly putting into progress the clean-up operation, when they realised that someone still wanted to take part. It was a man in a gorilla's outfit who had left home too late and had gone on a mad dash from the train station hoping to make it to the start in time. On he came, charging down the central motorway, and when he saw an official by the side of the course, without even hesitating, he handed his wallet over. "Could you look after this for me?" came the request.

Many problems find their way back to Coleby, who arrives at the finish well before the first runners get there. This year was no exception. The race had been a success and the clear-up operation was in progress long into the afternoon when a cry came up that there was a gorilla heading down the coast road.

Coleby stopped what he was doing. Just a short while earlier, he had been handed a wallet which was stuffed with money, credit cards, train tickets and a photo of the man with his children – and not a gorilla in sight. He had no idea whose it

The first year and I knew nothing about the impending Great North Run. At the time I was young and reasonably fit and a colleague at work asked me if I would enter the run to raise money for a charity. Liking a challenge, I duly entered, got accepted, and promptly forgot all about it. During a holiday with my girlfriend I announced that I was going to start training when we returned home. "No point," she answered, "we get home on Thursday and the run is on Sunday."

Anyway I turned up on Sunday suitably equipped in my Dunlop Green Flash sand-shoes and football shorts, but with a good suntan, and ran/jogged 13 miles. Unfortunately by the time I reached the finish they had run out of T-shirts (too many finishers) and I only had my medal to show for my efforts. I then hobbled my way to the ferry but not knowing South Shields I went the long way and walked about an additional 2 miles. It's fair to say I was knackered, but that night I was determined to go out. Every pub I went to was filled with Great North Run T-shirts - mine arrived in the post a couple of weeks later - and limping runners.

By 2003 I was part of the "elite" club and the Great North Run was my focal point of the year. Not long before the run my employer asked if I would go to our new offices in Trinidad and help them get set up. It sounded exotic so I obviously said yes. The problem was that this was two weeks before the run. I contacted Nova and they agreed that if I did not get back in time I could run the 13 miles in Trinidad and they would class it as still having completed the run. Off I went to Trinidad armed with my race number and running shoes.

I managed to get everything done by the Friday before the run so I caught the afternoon flight home. The flight took about 11 hours and, taking into account the time difference, I arrived in London around 9.00am on Saturday and Newcastle for about 1.00pm - all set for the run the following day. It's fair to say that run was probably the hardest ever. A combination of jet-lag, old age (not that old though) and lack of training all contributed to a very challenging run.

Michael Gowland, 24 not out!
47, Accountant, Cullercoats

1986

Perhaps the most unlikely star of 1986 was a fictitious plumber called Mario, the title character of the Super Mario Brothers game. This, the first video game from Nintendo, would eventually net its Japanese inventors an astonishing £3 billion. 1986 saw the birth of several more entertainment stalwarts. Andrew Lloyd Webber opened Phantom of the Opera and Aussie soap Neighbours brought the youthful Kylie Minogue to UK screens. Such popular and populist innovations were not confined to the media; the deregulation of the London Stock Market, christened 'Big Bang', had a huge effect on British life. Big Bang was intended to make the Conservative government's dream of a property owning democracy a reality by allowing small investors to buy shares more easily, but its side-effect was the creation of the Yuppie. This sub-class of British culture, easily identified by their Armani suits and Gucci loafer shoes, possessed large disposable incomes which began to fuel the biggest property boom for a generation. After April, however, the phrase Big Bang acquired a bitter irony when an explosion at a Soviet nuclear plant near Chernobyl sent a cloud of radioactive gas towards Western Europe.

1987

In March 1987 the Herald of Free Enterprise ferry capsized in Zeebrugge harbour, drowning 200 passengers and crew. In August, Michael Ryan, using an arsenal of legally held automatic weapons, shot dead 14 of his neighbours in the sleepy town of Hungerford. In October, while world leaders met in Montreal to sign a ground-breaking agreement limiting the use of ozone-depleting CFCs, a freak hurricane swept across South East England uprooting trees and causing widespread damage. Three days later, it was the turn of the world's stock markets to come crashing to the ground; Black Monday wiped billions off share values in London alone. The financial chaos was blamed on the failure of the automatic share-dealing computer programmes introduced after deregulation. Finally, as if to mark the passing of a gentler way of life, British Telecom announced that its famous red telephone boxes would be replaced by 'vandal proof plastic booths.

92, 93 What's your vice? Smoking, drinking or a plate of fried food? Go on. You deserve it... for once.

1987

WHEN Brendan Foster hears of stories about people who say the Great North Run has changed their lives, his smile widens. The way the Run has affected people never ceases to amaze him, but few are more special than Jim Purcell.

'Jarra Jim', as he has become known, is 84 this year, but he has run in every race since 1987. As his nickname suggests, he lives in Jarrow and he is one of the town's most popular faces, jogging to stay fit and never far from some kind of exercise to ensure that his body remains in trim. Incredibly, as he has grown older, he has actually started to run faster. In 2001, he finished the Great North Run in around four hours and 12 months later he clocked 3:40. "I was really delighted," he said.

In 1987 he did not expect all these years later to still be taking part, but the race provides a goal each year. His wife Betty died in 1982 and now the Great North Run is one way of alleviating the loneliness of this particular long distance runner.

"I switched on the telly and there was an item on about Gateshead Stadium and people jogging, and an interview with Brendan Foster. I thought: 'Could I? Have I found the answer?' I'll have a bash.

"Now where I live, the houses form a big circle, and it's about 500 yards all the way around. One night, waiting until it was dark, I quietly slipped out of the back door and I ran one complete circuit."

His love affair with jogging, and consequently the Great North Run, had begun.

It took over his life. He was too late to enter the 1986 race, but by 1987 he was ready. Jim Purcell was going to begin the first of his 17 Great North Runs – his life had found a direction.

His story was so engrossing that he wrote about it in a book of his own. The title could have become a slogan for the race 'It's the smiles that count'. In it, he tells of that first run and the pleasure the Great North has given him. He says in the book: "This is not a story of world records or championships, but of fun, friends, and something that changed my life and conquered that loneliness that as a retired widower I was about to endure."

A key part of his training was on one of the toughest sections of the course. He adds: "The John Reid Road was part of my run, and I remember watching the Great North Run on that road with my wife in 1981 when it first started. I thought then that one day I would like to run."

By 1987 he was in and with it came a fascinating insight to the masses of people that had gathered. He says: "I had never seen so many people gathered in one place since the beaches at Dunkirk. I was told it would be a bit daunting, 13 miles is a long way, but I had done the Geordie Run the year before so I wasn't too worried.

"As the time approached for the main body to start running, the excitement seemed to reach fever pitch, everyone talking to each other, jostling and joking, then the starting gun went off and we were away. Jog, stop, walk, we seemed to travel miles before we reached the actual start line and even then it wasn't until we had almost reached the Tyne Bridge that I could settle down.

"'The Tyne Bridge', the symbol of the Great North Run, I felt good. It is the ordinary, friendly chit-chat, fancy dress, and friendly support, that helps you along the way.

"I ran on, enjoying the atmosphere, and the crowd was uplifting. It was my first time but I resolved then it would not be my last. Approaching Heworth roundabout someone in the crowd must have recognised me. There was a loud shout: 'Jim keep going you old b*****d'. I don't mind what anyone calls me as long as it is not too early in the morning!

"At the Roman Road and Hadrian Road areas I came into my own, this is where I live, this is full of relatives, friends and neighbours. I felt six feet tall, there had to be a short stop and a chat now and again.

"The John Reid Road has a reputation of being a killer, undulating mostly uphill, and this after you have already run eight miles. I train in that area so I have a good idea how to approach it, the same way as I do the rest... slowly.

"Then I saw a figure in front of me, a black fellow in the Kenyan colours. I thought this is impossible, how could I catch up with one of those stars? Catch up I did... he was a big man, and I smiled, 'What part of Kenya do you come from?' I asked. 'Kenya! Kenya!' he said. 'I'm a miner, I've just come off the nightshift, I've never had time to have a shower. Kenya be blowed.'

"I finished in 2:10, happy I had made it."

But, as ever, his mind turned to a day 12 months ahead. This is a man who seldom stops thinking about, or living, the race that revived his world.

Jim Gibson

1988

THIS was the year when the profile of the BUPA Great North Run was raised beyond a Sunday fun run.

'Geordie Racer' has become a legendary show on children's BBC. It was part of the Look and Read series, which was shown on national television and even now is being repeated on CBBC, the corporation's network for youngsters.

The opening credits were sung by the children's television presenter, Derek Griffiths, and included the verse:

On the road, in the street,

Hear the sound of pounding feet,

Geordie racer, Geordie racer.

It encapsulated the mood of the North East. The show took great pride in its use of real-life locations around Newcastle. As the synopsis said, it was "emphasising 'good North East ingredients' such as pigeon fancying, stotty munching and the Great North Run – the aim being to ensure that there'll hardly be a child in the country who won't know exactly where Newcastle is."

This was achieved. In the 17 years since it was first shown, the Great North Run can now boast an entrant from every postcode in Britain. How many might have been attracted as children watching a show that cast the real-life husband-and-wife actors Kevin Whately and Madelaine Newton? The main character was a child called Spuggy Hilton, while Peter Rowell was a genuine Radio Newcastle DJ with a local issues call-in show.

During the series, Whately and Spuggy's sister, Cath, manage to run two miles of the 13.1-mile route of the Great North Run, and their journey is faithful to the course itself. This was actually carefully planned – the running scenes were filmed several months after the rest of the story had been completed, during the 1987 Great North Run on Sunday June 21.

Michael Steele/Getty Images

Stock footage of the run was drawn from the BBC's own recorded coverage of the event. For advice on filming, the production team went to see charity run veteran Jimmy Savile, who revealed that he employed a team of accomplices to run behind and around him to act as crowd control. 'Geordie Racer' did the same, so when the heroes burst into the crowd of runners, they were not really getting in the way of innocent athletes, but acting out a carefully choreographed scene."

It was fabulous fiction, and fantastic, all-year-round publicity for the Run.

1988 also saw a major expansion of the whole event. Following a change in the composition of the field of runners for the main Run (under-16s could no longer take part because the Amateur Athletic Association had incorporated the Great North Run as their national half-marathon championships), the organisers had first planned for a Junior Run over the same course, beginning after the elite runners had started on their way.

This arrangement was deemed too confusing, and so the original one-day event was greatly expanded to become a multi-event festival over two weekends, with the Great North Walk and the Great North Bike Ride as the first two events, held on the preceding Saturday and Sunday respectively. The following Saturday, the Great Junior Run took place, starting and finishing at Gateshead Stadium; with the Great North Run the next day, on Sunday.

94, 95 Everybody needs a helping hand. Running with loved ones, friends or something more fruity perhaps?

1988

The British love an heroic failure and the 1988 Winter Olympics provided the most famous of all when Eddie 'The Eagle' Edwards confounded his critics by surviving the ski jump events unscathed. Britons who made the trip to Canada to support the unlikely hero had to carry the red EU passports introduced this year but those who mourned the loss of the famous blue booklets could at least comfort themselves by collecting British Airway's new Airmiles. The year also produced two unlikely fashion icons. The first were T-shirts featuring a yellow 'smiley face' badge that caused consternation thanks to the symbol's association with 'Acid House' drug culture. The second was a red plastic clown nose sold to raise money for the first Comic Relief telethon. Sadly, the laughter stopped in December after another terrorist atrocity: at 7.19 pm a bomb exploded on Pan Am flight 103 causing the airliner to crash on to the small Scottish town of Lockerbie. Nearly 300 people were killed.

1989

SINCE the start of the race, the number of celebrity runners has grown. Sir Jimmy Savile, the legendary radio DJ and television personality, had become a regular – not just here but in London as well – while John Motson, the BBC football commentator, had run it in 1983 and 1987. But more celebrities wanted to take part – with the resultant increase in television coverage, the profile of the Run was being raised again.

Ray Scott had run in all eight previous races. He was a friend of Brendan Foster from Gateshead Harriers. They used to train together on a Tuesday night and Scott had embraced this biggest athletics occasion in the North East.

Foster asked if Scott would like to look after the celebrities – from the moment the gun fires to the time they decide to go home. He jumped at the chance.

So, now, if you are watching the race, and you wonder how the BBC know that former national hunt jockey Richard Dunwoody is in the home straight or that interviewer Sally Gunnell has stopped football pundit Mark Lawrenson for a chat after six miles, it is not by luck that they have been spotted. It is by clever planning.

Scott has a team of 25 runners from the local athletics club – some who can run as fast as 1:15, others a bit slower, but all 10 minutes faster than the celebrities' personal best – to chaperone the personalities.

They wear fluorescent yellow jackets – so they stand out to the television cameras – and when they enter the last mile, a military-style operation begins, to ensure that the BBC and organisers know that a famous name is on their way.

But not all celebrities want to talk on the way – some are there to run serious times, such as Dunwoody, chef Gordon Ramsay and Tony Audenshaw (Bob Hope) from Emmerdale, who in 2004 broke the Run's celebrity record of 1:26, by one minute. It was the time Kevin Keegan had set in the first race in 1981.

Scott continues: "You find some people who are going for a time will do interviews at the start and finish but none during the Run. Then you have other people like Chris Chittell (Eric Pollard) from Emmerdale, who will do whatever you ask.

"We try to get the guys running with celebrities with whom they might have similar interests. For

96, 97 *Water, water everywhere and plenty to drink. The wonderful work of the Scouts and others is one of the reasons the Great North Run is such a success.*

example, the Yorkshire cricket player David Byas ran one year. One of the lads is a cricket nut, so they ran together. There is a good camaraderie between the celebrities and the chaperones.

"We do what the celebrity wants – if they need a post-run medical treatment we take them, but if they want a beer we go with them too."

The numbers grow each year, and since 1989 the impact of the celebrity has reached a level which has also helped to increase the amount of money raised for charity. Many of the celebrities have run for Leukaemia Research – not just in the Great North but other BUPA events and the Flora London Marathon – and they range from soap opera stars from Heartbeat and The Bill to celebrity chefs. They all wear yellow shirts, they are known as the Banana Army – in 2003 there were 5,000 people in these colours running for Leukaemia Research – and alongside the famous faces, in another shade of the same colour, were the unknown runners who play their own special, and equally important, part.

I entered my First GNR in June 1983. I was going to enter in 1982 but found out you had to pay a fee! Pay money for all that pain? No thanks! Anyway, my next-door neighbour ran and so did a bloke over the back. He was a REAL runner. He spent the outlandish amount of £45 on his shoes (720S if memory serves me right) – and he belonged to a club, Houghton Harriers. He had the shortest shorts and the longest legs I had ever seen. He never wore Ron Hill 'tights', even in the depths of winter. He came in from a 'quick 15 miler' one night when we'd had a heavy snowfall. The temperature must have been about -7°C. He had frost on his eyebrows + his sweat had frozen in droplets on the ends of the hairs on his legs. Boy, was I impressed.

"Come out for a little jog," these two said one sunny August day in 1982. So, on the strength of having done a bit of running for rugby training, I laced on my trusty £5 trainers and went.

They left me! We were only two miles into a six mile 'little jog'. I shuffled back with blisters on my blisters. I couldn't move for a week! But something stirred. I knew back then that this would become a lifelong endeavour. I ran the 1983 GNR and, with training, managed to get my times down over the years to a modest 1:30:09.

And, I'm still doing it. I've only missed two GNR's in that time – 1998 to get my left knee fixed and 2003 with a pulled tendon. I was going to make 2004 my last as it was number 20, and it had become more 'Great North Limp' than Run, but then a member of my school staff who removes the bar codes at the finish remarked that 2005 would be the Silver Anniversary GNR and my 21st. My God! I've come of age and I can't even remember hitting puberty!

See you for 21 of 25 on the day. Stroll on Marra's!

Barry Lumsdon
54, Deputy Head Teacher, Jarrow

1989

The Cold War's Iron Curtain was finally lifted in 1989. Mikhail Gorbachev's withdrawal of Soviet troops from Afghanistan and the softening of his foreign policy in Eastern Europe unleashed an unstoppable tide of popular revolt against Soviet-style communism. From the Baltic to the Black Sea, the former Eastern Bloc opened its borders to the West; in Berlin, the infamous Wall was pulled down amid scenes of wild jubilation and in Czechoslovakia the dissident poet Vaclav Havel was swept to power by the 'Velvet Revolution'. In Poland, rebel trade union Solidarity formed a government while in the Balkans the communist regimes of Yugoslavia, Bulgaria and Romania disintegrated, apparently overnight. Back in Britain, football hooliganism was back at the top of the political agenda after a 'crowd surge' crushed 96 Liverpool fans to death at Sheffield's Hillsborough Stadium. In the countryside too, the police seemed powerless to prevent huge crowds gathering as revellers flocked to the increasingly popular, but illegal, music festivals known as 'raves'.

98, 99 *Expectation and exhilaration. At the finish (98) or at the start (99) the one emotion is the forerunner of the other.*

Bryn Lennon/Getty Images

1990

THE race reached its 10th anniversary this year and, to celebrate, a special documentary was made, looking back on the previous decade. It was called 'Eric, You Must Be Barmy'. This title was based on a banner raised by a member of the crowd in one of the early races, it was tongue-in-cheek and appealed to the ordinary person running. Why would they want to run, jog or walk 13.1 miles?

It was a question that Stan Long, Brendan Foster's former coach and lifelong friend, would answer every time a new person came to his regular 'Lunchtime' training sessions at Gateshead Stadium, which by now were at the height of their popularity.

Long was one of the great characters of the race, and of North East folklore. How sad it is that in 2005 he died just a matter of months before the 25th race. It is impossible to gauge the number of people he had helped on the way.

But it was in 1990, during the television show about the run, that Mike Neville, the North East's leading television personality, gave him his nickname. He dubbed him 'Wilson of The Wizard', after the sports superstar created by the 'Wizard' adventure comic between 1922-63. Of the apparently immortal Wilson it was said: 'Wilson's all-round sports achievements in his black woollen bodysuit had amazed the world.'

Long had a way about him that endeared runners to him at his training sessions. He had coached Brendan Foster to world records at Two Miles and 3,000 metres, and to Olympic 10,000m bronze in Montreal in 1976.

Neville said in 1990: "One of the things about his training sessions was that you would have all these businessmen running behind the girls, whose skirts were fluttering in the wind. It certainly increased the interest and the numbers!"

John Caine says of Long: "Stan, generously, freely, unselfishly and equally, gave of his time to talented, untalented, young and old . Without doubt the highest achievers to benefit from his guidance and advice were Brendan Foster and Charlie Spedding (1984 London Marathon winner) but he gained immense pleasure and pride encouraging anyone interested in being a runner.

"Working as a welder at a local engineering company, Stan was recruited by Gateshead Council to work at the refurbished Gateshead Stadium in 1975. His brief was simple – get people interested in running and using the track . This he did famously, with breakfast, lunchtime and evening sessions for anyone and everyone.

Bryn Lennon/Getty Images

"His outgoing and friendly personality made him a natural candidate as host for the national and international press corps which started attending Stadium events. Just as with his runners, all were treated equally and warmly welcomed, although they were often puzzled by his accent and famous misspellings of difficult foreign athletes' names!

"Everyone left with the same impression – what a wonderful ambassador for Gateshead and the sport of running."

Long was asked for some of his best Great North Run stories. He realised that however hard and however well he advised the runners, they might not always listen. On the days of the Run, Long did his best to help them keep their minds on the race. He said: "Before the start I would laugh and talk with other runners. I would tell them not to do anything stupid – though I saw one runner drink a bottle of milk and by the time he got half a mile it must have curdled in his stomach. It would practically be butter."

The 1998 Great North Run was my first half-marathon and I've done them all since in fancy dress.

Miles 1 & 2 were downhill bliss, miles 3 to 12 were uphill woe, mile 13 an everlasting prom and then the thrill of the finish line. Feeling like you can go no further, weighed down with your medal and bag of swag you stand in utter delight to say, 'Yes! I did it!'.

At the blink of an eye, it's 2005, and I find myself in line for my 8th Great North Run. There is something special in the air of Tyne and Wear, which makes you return year after year.

Still turning out in fancy dress, nothing beats the Geordie yell of, 'Well done pet!'

Christine Edwards
29, Payroll Manager, Powys

1990

The last decade of the 'People's Century' opened with a wave of triumph for 'people power'. Enormous international pressure forced the South African government to release Nelson Mandela from prison, East and West Germany were reunited and the Soviet Union began to dissolve into its constituent states. In Britain, widespread riots sounded the death knell for the Conservative's deeply unpopular poll tax, introduced to finance local government, and the unrest eventually forced the resignation of prime minister Margaret Thatcher. New prime minister John Major announced the pound would enter the European Exchange Rate Mechanism and our geographical isolation ended, for the first time since the Ice Age, when Great Britain was once more joined to continental Europe by the Channel Tunnel. Yet closer ties to Europe did not prevent the French government introducing a ban on British beef after the BSE scare. 'Mad Cow Disease', caused by using infected sheep carcasses as cattle feed, led to the culling of thousands of British cows.

SALLY GUNNELL

my part in it...

Former European, World, Commonwealth and Olympic 400m hurdles Champion.

I well remember running the race in 2001 and it was a memorable occasion for me. Although I had done little fun runs before, I had never been involved in the bigger runs and saw this as a big challenge. There were three main reasons:

First of all it was a personal challenge as I had never run such a long distance before. The fun runs had just been a few miles. Now here I was going to run a half-marathon.

Second, I knew it would be a good idea to help me get back into shape after the birth of my middle child (Luca) and that encouraged me to get properly prepared.

And finally, as I said, I had no experience of mass participation races. Everyone was also telling what a great experience it would be and so it proved.

I was lucky in that they gave me a great guy to run with (Ray Scott) and I said to him he had to keep talking with me all of the way to help me along, which he did. It was hard going at times and I stopped in the showers along the course when I could to cool down. My plan was to churn out eight-minute miles and I must say the encouragement of the crowd lining the route was absolutely fantastic. They were cheering me on all of the way, shouting my name – it was an incredible atmosphere.

Coming towards the end of the race and up the final hill, I started feeling great thinking it was all was over. But it wasn't. I then had to push my body along the final stretch of the coast road and that was a long, long, way. I'd never sworn after a race before, but when crossing the finishing line I did.

Yet it was such fun. I had achieved a personal ambition and although I cannot fit it in this year – the BBC won't give me time off – I'll certainly be back in the future.

I have now completed every Great North Run and intend to do as many as my body allows me. People often ask why I started running and it was because of the Great North Run. I worked in the shop floor of the Caterpillar Tractor factory based in Birtley. My friend Alan Phillipson was promoted to a staff position and ended up working upstairs in an office job.

Two years later I was promoted and went to work upstairs in the same office. Alan by then had put on a lot of weight and he said to me, "You'd better keep fit, otherwise you will end up putting a lot of weight on like me." Shortly after that he came in to work one day and said he had seen an advert in the Evening Chronicle for a race called the Great North Run. He said that he and I should train up and enter it. I said, 'That sounds good. How far is it?' When he told me it was 13.1 miles I said, 'Don't be stupid. I can't run that far!' At the time I thought I was fit because I was running five miles a week at the weekend. Needless to say we did the training following the official training programme. Alan lost weight and we both completed the first ever Great North Run.

Alan and I went on to run many marathons, including the London Marathon; we then went on to do several mini Triathlons. Even now, twenty five years later, I still train every day, more so now to keep fit and I do not do as many races as I used to. Now, however, my daughter comes out running with me; I think that was one of Brendan's objectives at the beginning – to get the North East running and to become fitter people.

Dennis Thynne
Stanley, County Durham

100, 101 Time waits for no man – elite or otherwise – and to many runners it is the key to one's achievement.

1991

AS the race moved into its second decade, now becoming the street party that the North East people as well as the founders wanted it to be, a problem emerged. The Run was scheduled for Sunday September 15th – and six days beforehand, with the organisers already beginning to ready the course, the area became headline news, for all the wrong reasons.

Across the river in North Shields two young joy riders were killed in a police chase. It led to two nights of rioting on an estate, the Meadow Well. Suddenly the race itself seemed in doubt; not because trouble was forecast, but would it have been proper to stage the Run so close to what had happened, and would the police allow it? Would they have enough officers to man the route? They generally commissioned 170 for the race, but many had been dispatched in the attempt to quell the problems that had exploded – literally – with fire bombs and looting.

"We have precautions for every situation," says Brendan Foster. "But we would only want to put these plans into action if there was no other option."

The organisers waited anxiously to hear if they would be advised to cancel. But the riots ended, the Run would go ahead and on the Friday beforehand, at a press conference, television celebrity Jimmy Savile gave his opinion: "It is now time to show the world what this area is really all about."

In the week of the Great North Run, for once it was not the race that had caught the media attention. But the organisers considered that their Run would be as important as it ever had been to lift people's spirits.

It worked a treat.

There was also news in 1991 that in a year's time the Great North Run would incorporate the first World Half-Marathon Championships, but Foster stressed that the essence of the Run would not be lost: "Next year might be an important – even historic – occasion. But the man in the street will not be forgotten. The inclusion of international runners from over 180 countries affiliated to the International Amateur Athletic Federation will provide a brilliant spectacle, but their presence will not be allowed to interfere with the needs of the fun runner. The Great North Run belongs to the people of the North East."

Each year, the race would change in some way. More bands were being introduced on to the course to keep the runners' spirits up while the VIP area also increased each year. But in 1991, the introduction of a separate race for elite women was the most significant change.

Instead of everyone running together, the women started 10 minutes before the men. It added hugely to the profile of the women's race and made the job of the BBC infinitely easier. For the spectators who lined the streets it also made the event easier to follow – no longer were the female runners lost within the posse of men.

The big clash was expected to be between Ingrid Kristiansen, the marathon world record holder and fabulous distance star from Norway, and Jill Hunter, the British international from Newcastle. The women's race was superb, with Kristiansen winning, but it was finally another Briton, Andrea Wallace, who came through to take second with Hunter in third place.

Today, with the presence of runners like Paula Radcliffe, the women's race, whose future had at one point looked in doubt, has now developed into arguably a more competitive and popular event than the male elite equivalent.

102, 103 Horses for courses, and dogs, and the dining room chairs, and the... you'll see it all.

1991

Kuwait was liberated in just three days after an international coalition of forces launched a land offensive, named Operation Desert Storm, on February 24th. But as the smart bombs and laser guided guns of the First Gulf War fell silent, the opening shots were fired in another conflict as the former Yugoslavian states of Bosnia, Croatia and Serbia fell upon each other in an orgy of civil strife. In Britain, troops returning from the Gulf suddenly found themselves being able to shop for seven days a week as supermarkets openly flouted the ban on Sunday trading and the newspapers were full of the news that Robert Maxwell, the media tycoon, had drowned after falling from his yacht. Maxwell's death revealed a web of financial deceit and the chaos of his companies' pension funds was mirrored by the parlous state of the British economy; unemployment stood at 2.5 million and repossessions of houses reached a record 80,000 per year.

1992

THE growth of the race has been remarkable, and much of it has to do with the success of sponsorship. By luck or judgement, by 2009, when their current deal runs out, BUPA will have been sponsors of the Run for 17 years, which is arguably one of the longest relationships in the sports world.

Since BUPA became the sponsors, they have ploughed millions into the Great North Run, allowing it to expand. Rarely has there been a sponsorship where event and sponsor have worked so effectively together.

Thorn EMI Gas Heating was the first sponsor and backed the race for the opening four years. But in 1985, Pearl Assurance, one of Britain's biggest insurance companies, was the prime sponsor of athletics in Britain. Part of their package saw them become involved in the Great North Run. By 1989, the Pearl Assurance agreement was over and the race was left without a sponsor. "We were struggling," says Dave Roberts, once the man responsible for the race's start, now the sponsorship manager. Diet Coke was an emerging product and they needed a way of promoting it. "The Great North Run hit the right button," says Roberts. The major stumbling block was that the race was only in Newcastle. Coca-Cola UK, who produce Diet Coke, wanted a national presence. Consequently, the birth of the series of 'Great' races took place.

By 1989, the Great North Run had grown in size – there were well over 29,000 entries – and in six months, the Great series was developed: the Great Midland Run, the Great Scottish Run, the Great Welsh Run, the Great South Run, the Great London Run, and, finally, the Great North Run as the last meeting on the programme.

With the financial backing that Coca-Cola UK provided, Nova were able to present packages to regional councils and it became very much like a travelling family. The local areas would arrange the races, and Nova would move in on the week of the event to set it up alongside them.

By 1991, the growth of the Great North Run was steadily increasing and in addition more half-marathons were springing up around the world. Brendan Foster had an idea. How about a World Half-Marathon Championship? Contact was made with the sport's international governing body, the International Amateur Athletic Association (IAAF), and they liked the idea. The IAAF's

World Outdoor Championships were moving from a four-year cycle to every two years, as the President, the Italian Primo Nebiolo, wanted to promote the sport more and further enhance the profile of its events.

The World Half-Marathon would become part of the Great North Run. It seemed a clever idea at the time, but, it has been said, it led to dwindling numbers for the race in the years that followed because it over-emphasised the elite aspect of the event. 1992 was a vintage year. Liz McColgan, of Scotland, won the women's event and Benson Masya, of Kenya, won his second of four Great North Runs. The decision to stage the World Half-Marathon as part of the Great North Run was one of the first steps to BUPA coming on board.

As deals were beginning to be struck to stage the World Half-Marathon championships, a problem occurred. One of the main sponsors of the IAAF were Coca-Cola Worldwide, which put them in direct competition with Coca-Cola UK. International Sports Limited (ISL), the advertising arm of the IAAF, stepped in.

Roberts says: "We were told by ISL that we could not have the name Diet Coke displayed on the start gantry because it contravened the marketing strategy of Coca-Cola worldwide. It was watering down their branding opportunity."

A number of the top ranking officials from the IAAF became involved. "We were looking after our client, Coca-Cola UK," explains Roberts. "We got what we wanted in the end. The IAAF agreed. However, it had tainted the sponsorship and we got the warning signs that the Diet Coke deal could be coming to an end." They were right.

The contract was up for renewal and Diet Coke decided they wanted to move away from sport and into leisure marketing. Before they had officially told Nova, Roberts had put the wheels into motion for another sponsorship package.

Within a week, BUPA said they were interested. Their Managing Director Roger Hyam liked the idea of the link with the Run. People need to get into shape and the practical health implications all married in well. At the start of 1993 the race became known as the BUPA Great North Run. It was the beginning of a great relationship.

104, 105 Paws for thought... There are a wealth of charities to run for, and the beneficiaries? You, them... all of us

I have competed in all of the Great North Runs to date, despite our move to Harrogate, and each run is a family affair for us. My dad has done all but four of the runs. Each of my children runs in the Great North Run and we have a back-up team of loyal family members who get us to the start line and back home afterwards.

There was one year, however, when we left getting our bags to the bag bus — and then missed the bus. The prospect of my dad and I having to run to South Shields with a bag on our backs did not appeal. I decided to knock on the door at one of the terraced houses near the start and beg for our bags to be left and we would collect them in the evening. The little old man who answered the door was only too pleased to help — as I left the bags with him he was almost crushed by 15-20 bags thrown in over my shoulder! I had not realised that behind me was a queue of people all with the same idea but they weren't waiting to ask. When we got back in the evening he had lined all the bags up in his hallway in alphabetical order and was supervising the collection. We all owed him a lot and still reminisce each year about this.

Gary Warriner
45, Solicitor, Knaresborough

1993

SURELY there has never been a story like that of Johnny Waughman. He is 54, a musician from Essex and a friend of British Olympian Daley Thompson. He runs for fun and when the cannon fired to signal the start of the1993 BUPA Great North Run, he got shot!

The fact that he now laughs about it is probably as good a reflection of the spirit of the race as any. So what did actually happen? He opens his shirt to reveal a scar on his chest. A war wound from the world's biggest half-marathon.

In 1993, Waughman had been friendly with Britain's double Olympic decathlon champion, for 11 years. They had met when Thompson was at the height of his fame.

Thompson was not an endurance athlete. His forte was his powerful explosiveness from the blocks, the speed he used in the sprints and on the runways of the field events that had brought him world acclaim. Waughman has run the London Marathon on 12 occasions.

By 1993, he had agreed to run the Great North with Thompson – but only for four miles because he had a gig in London that evening and would not be back in time if he completed the whole course. He could never have predicted that he would not even make it across the start line.

Charity events play a big part in Thompson's life and in 1993 such an occasion took him to Newcastle. The atmosphere was typical: a glorious day with a huge crowd. Waughman met Sir Bobby Charlton, who was there as one of the guests, and he will never forget what the occasion was like.

"I was looking back down the field, thinking to myself this was fantastic," he recalls. "It was so impressive."

The warm-ups had finished and the race was seconds away. In front of him was a field including the likes of elite runner Moses Tanui, of Kenya; Waughman and Thompson were positioned to the left of the start, close by the edge of the road.

Pointing away from the runners, for obvious reasons, was the official starting mechanism. It had been a tradition for the army to bring their cannon to start the race because the noise could alert more than 20,000 people in one go.

Thompson and Waughman were ready. Boom, boom! The gun went off. Waughman is not quite sure what happened next, except he remembers

John Williamson

BANANAS FOR SHOES.
ONE DAY ONLY
OFFER DOES
NOT APPLY
TO SANDALS.
BANISH UGLY
TRAINERS

GREAT NORTH

Ad Infinitum

"But I was lying there and of course no one had any sympathy! They have such a great sense of humour up there and I remember this bloke going past saying: 'Aye lad, the race ain't even started yet,' and then every ten people that went past me would say something."

Somehow he was not trodden or trampled on, and, amid the crowd, he managed to climb to his feet – in a daze.

"I looked at this soldier, who put his hands up, all but saying it was nothing to do with him but it was!" he adds.

Thompson, meanwhile, was nowhere to be seen. Caught up in the charge of the race, he was well into the first mile by now, unaware of what had happened to his friend and with no way of turning back with 20,000 people following him.

As he climbed to his feet Waughman thought he had only one option. He would go home. He says: "As I was only going to run the first four miles, I was holding my wallet and other things. I decided to go home straight away, despite the fact I had blood running down me and was in a state of shock."

He was more dazed than in pain. He made his way through to the side of the course, and meandered back to Newcastle Central Station, took the first train to London and without seeking hospital treatment, he headed home.

"I don't know why I didn't go to hospital," he says now. "I cleaned the blood up, but I must have looked some sight on the train. That night I went to the concert. I told the guys that I had been shot by a cannon. It sounded pretty impressive.

"Daley loves to tell the story and rumour has it that when he got to the finish, he just asked 'Where's Johnny?'."

Thompson also had a great story from the day. He was struggling near the finish and had to go into a local sweetshop for some sustenance. The owner was so surprised to see him that she gave him a Mars bar!

Thankfully Waughman lives to tell the tale, but as he says, it could have been so different. "It might have hit me in the eye," he says. But he never had any intention of taking action against the organisers. "I should have sued," he says, with a huge grin on his face. "But no-one would have wanted anything like that."

106-109 Telling you how it is... do you really need these guy's verbal abuse (page 106, 107) – well tough, you're going to get it! Others have a simpler message.

looking up from a prostrate position on the floor with people streaming past him.

He says: "We had all been limbering up, with this sense of excitement, ready for the race. The cannon went off and I was just rooted to the floor. My legs were shaking a bit, I felt a sensation around me but I did not know what was wrong. I looked at my shirt, there was nothing there. I put my hand under my shirt and there was blood."

What had happened was that after the race had been started, a second shell had been released from the gun and a tiny piece of wadding had flown into the air, hitting Waughman. It was the freakiest of flukes.

He continues: "It did not even go through the shirt. My hands were trembling, I was shaking, but of course the race had started. I fell to the floor and I must have been there for two minutes. Have a think about how many runners can go past you in that time.

1994

ONE of the main talking points for many athletics fans is the statistical figures that envelop the sport. They can make fascinating reading. Times change; heights and distances and world records improve over the years. However, when the 1994 BUPA Great North Run was over, and Nova began digesting the after-effects of the race, the statistics did not make very pleasant reading.

It had been the 14th staging of the Run and there were more people who failed to show up on the day than ever before. There had been 27,383 entrants, of which 27.9 per cent were 'no-shows'. Amazingly, even with only 847 more entries than the previous year, the 'no-shows' were up by 5.9 per cent. The BUPA Great North Run was facing its biggest crisis.

What was the best way to deal with a decline in runners, when there seemed no obvious reason? Looking at the figures, it could be seen that the number slid down from the 33,485 who had entered in 1991 to 27,383 in 1994.

Nova decided one way to find out why this was happening was to ask the people themselves. Two thousand letters were sent out to runners who had appeared in 1993 but not 1994 and another batch were distributed to people who had run in both.

John Caine recalls the outcome:

"We surveyed a cross-section of people and we got a great response, about 1,200 replies, and they nearly all said the same thing. They thought the fun had been taken out of the run."

It stemmed back to 1992, the year that the race incorporated the World Half-Marathon championships. That was the first year where there had been a drop in numbers, and the general perception was that the run's priority was more about elite racing than the ordinary person jogging in the street.

Caine adds: "There was a question and answer section on the survey and a space for an opinion. When we got everything back, the strong message that was coming through was that people were not interested in world championships or Kenyans breaking world records. They were interested in having fun, raising money, having a bloody good day out and doing it for their own fitness."

Nova took their views on board – and changes were made.

John Williamson

"We sat down and thought 'How can we make it more fun?'," continues Caine. "We decided to introduce Mr Motivator to give people a warm-up routine before the race with his aerobics. We developed the Bands on the Run and increased the amount of entertainment along the course. We started promoting the charities more heavily and we had a photographic competition for the best fancy-dressed runner. We started to give people more of what they wanted."

While Nova accepted that the World Championships in 1992 probably did not work in their favour as much as they had hoped, they did ultimately lead to the arrival of BUPA as the Run's main sponsor and put the race's name on the world map because of the championship link.

But of course, sometimes a decline can be hard to stop and the next year the numbers dropped again, when 25,566 entries were received. But on the day, the 'no-shows' were down to 24.3 per cent. By 1996, entries were back up again – well above 32,000 – and by the year 2000 the size of the race entry was a massive 50,000 plus and the run had been totally reinvigorated..

The Great North Run was my first tangible target as a 38 year old novice fun runner. My concerns related to the distance, and whether I could complete it. However, I made it to the finish line. I have run for a number of charities and in one particular year I collected money in a bucket from people lining the route. I staggered to the finish and can verify that a bucket full of money weighs many kilograms! I would like to thank the crowds of onlookers who watch the Great North Run.

Since 1981 I have remained a non-smoker and have never sustained an injury which has prevented me from undertaking each of the 24 Great North Runs.

Since our retirement, my wife and I spend several months during the winter living on the West Bank of Luxor in Egypt. I continue to run 3-4 times a week and this always seems unusual to Egyptians who are not noted for their commitment in great numbers towards running and athletics. They shake their heads, and regularly say that I shouldn't be 'wearing my legs out'.

Keith Hamilton
63, Retired, Mickley, Northumberland

RAY STUBBS *my part in it...*

Presenter for Grandstand, Match of the Day and Final Score.

When offered an audience with Lord Foster of Northumberland some seven or eight years ago, the invitation to take part in the Great North Run was hard to turn down. Brendan has a clever way of asking yet challenging you, a little grin appears on his face as he says 'that's if you're able to manage it mind'. Very clever, playing on the competitive spirit. Since then it's been a fixture on my racing calendar although it's the only fixture on my racing calendar. On one hand there's the immense sense of personal achievement you get when you cross the finish line; when you reach South Shields and go down that hill it's a real buzz, although those with experienced legs are well aware that when you turn the corner there's still a mile to go; you see the sea, think you're home, you have to gather yourself for one last mile.

The health issue is a big thing for me, The Great North Run is the vehicle that helps me keep some small semblance of fitness: age, ability, size issues can be put to one side, it's you against yourself or you against anyone you like, make it as competitive as you like. Much more important, you feel you're taking part in something that is doing good; just by being there, enjoying great north-east hospitality, you feel part of something that is making such a positive contribution. A moving mass of humanity goes from Newcastle to South Shields and you feel proud to be in the field.

It's a very personal thing too, my friend and colleague Mark Lawrenson ran in memory of a sister a few years ago, didn't make a fuss, didn't do any training by the way, but from scratch ran a half-marathon, raised some money for a great cause. So when you're shattered at 9 miles you get perspective when someone goes past you with a T-shirt that says 'For you Grandad'. The 4 remaining miles might not get much easier but they're worth doing, it doesn't matter how quickly. Add up the millions raised via the Great North Run, it's a fantastic event.

You make great mates thanks to the Great North Run. I have run alongside two Gateshead Harriers every year. Dave Leng and Steve English help me every inch of the way, there is a great camaraderie out on the course. Dave and Steve have to go in first or second gear but we have a great laugh. It's several years ago now but I can claim to have introduced them to Vodka and Red Bull at a post race party down on the Quayside – it had been pints of Guinness for those two Geordies – I think they thought it was pop, they were all for running home till I calmed them down.

You don't really get it at the time but when you look back at the TV pictures afterwards and see the helicopter shot of the field moving from the start you begin to appreciate the scale of the event. This is a world-class race, world champions in the field and you are in the same race. They don't let you join in at the back in a Formula One Grand Prix!

One year I was on the train the day after the race. A young lad was sitting opposite me. "Did you run yesterday?" he asked. "Yes," I replied. "How did you go?" he asked. "Not great, 2:02," I explained. When this fit youngster said he had run 1:58 I didn"t feel that bad, I could give him 20 years and he had beaten me by only four minutes. Just as I was starting to tell myself there was life in the old dog yet, he said, "Mind you, the big Rhino suit does get in the way a bit!" I limped away towards the buffet car but got cramp!

It should be stressed that Brendan Foster is the architect of something that has generated something that is just so good. It is a vehicle that has brought about so much good it's impossible to measure… way over 13 million miles of good!

110-113 Sign of the times. It doesn't matter what you're doing, everyone's support is more than welcome as those muscles begin to tighten.

1995

WERE you there making history? For once this had nothing to do with record times or runners being shot on the start line! The 27,000 people who entered the BUPA Great North Run also entered the Guinness Book of World Records when, prior to the start of the race, they joined in the world's biggest get-fit session. Led by television personality Mr Motivator, the numbers in the Run broke the world record of 26,017 which had been set in South Korea two years before.

The BBC coverage increased this year to three hours, while the runners were started on their way by Jonathan Edwards, the triple jump world champion and world record holder who lives locally. They set off on their 13.1 mile journey to the tune of the Blaydon Races which was played by the Pegswood Brass Band from Northumberland.

But it was at the finish where the biggest change took place as Lindisfarne topped the bill in a carnival show at Gypsies Green in South Shields. The Run was fast becoming become the Great North Party too – and unlike today, it was an afternoon event.

Now, in 2005, the new tradition is for it to be in the morning, but in 1995 the race did not begin until 12.35pm – with the Great Junior Run at 10am. Nowadays, the Great North Junior Run takes place the day before – and in recent years it has been followed by a pop concert with some of the country's leading chart stars and the whole event has been shown live on the BBC's children's channels. From Lindisfarne to Girls Aloud...

Scotland's Liz McColgan won the women's race and Moses Tanui, of Kenya, won the men's, but the event was struck by tragedy when Ian Graham, 35, from Washington, collapsed moments after crossing the finishing line and later died.

In the build-up to the run, the talk had grown about the race actually moving away from Tyneside. In July, it was revealed by The Journal that one local council had approached Nova International suggesting that the run could be switched to 'freshen it up'.

Whitley Bay, Tynemouth, Sunderland and Chester-Le-Street were all possible sites for the finishing line – and other ideas were that it might even be moved to Leeds or Manchester.

But as McColgan triumphed for Britain in South Shields, the Great North organisers revealed that the event would not be leaving the North East.

Foster said: "Whatever happens, the race will always cross the Tyne Bridge. We might consider running it the other way or turning left or right and going to Sunderland or Gateshead. But these are the only options. It won't move out of the North East."

We ever-presents are trapped by the fear of dropping out of the elite "EVERY RUN BRIGADE!" In January 2001, I herniated two discs in my lower spine. My right foot was useless; I had violent pins and needles from buttock to knee and no feeling at all below the knee. Being off work for five months, it required a complex operation and extensive physiotherapy to put it right. Two days before the Run, my neurosurgeon gave me the all clear to resume my life.

"Does this mean I can do the Run?"

"Are you mad!" he replied

I intended to just walk the course, but once the excitement took hold I thought that at least I would run to the Tyne Bridge. What happened was that I managed to hobble the first 10 miles before I started to walk, totally taken over by the atmosphere. I eventually started running again as I turned on to the coast road and crossed the line in a time of 2 hours 17 minutes.

My wife went absolutely mad when she heard what I had done. She had refused to come and watch from her usual location. Being 48 years old at the time, she thought I was too old anyway. Now I am in my 52nd year and the 25th run is approaching. How many other ever-presents have been through the same agonies at the thought of missing out on the record of every run? I bet there are quite a few!

John Brampton
South Shields

Ad Infinitum

1996

BENSON MASYA crossed the line with a smile. It would be the last time that the race's most prolific winner would be triumphant – and seven years later he would be dead at the age of just 33.

Duncan Mackay, athletics correspondent of The Guardian and Observer, tells his story, one that ended in tragedy.

Benson Masya never achieved world records or world titles and will not go down in history as one of the all-time greats of African runners. But he should have done.

On four occasions Masya won the Great North Run – in 1991, 1992, 1994, and here in the Olympic year of 1996. He also won the Honolulu Marathon three times and in 1992 and 1994 was widely considered by a number of athletics magazines in Britain and America to be the best road-runner in the world. His run of eight victories in 11 races spread over a 13 week period in 1994 on the ultra-tough American road racing circuit was unprecedented in the history of the sport.

It earned Benson the nickname 'The Tyson of the Tarmac' in recognition of his former sporting life as a bantamweight boxer in Kenya's Postal Service. Masya found the punishment of running less striking than that of boxing, though he brought many of the pugilist's traits to his racing. He often used to go to the front of races in an aggressive manner and dared the competition to follow. The manner in which he rolled his shoulders was reminiscent of someone ducking and diving on the ropes to ensure the competition could never hurt him. When he was on form, rivals rarely went the distance with him.

But sadly, as is the case for many homesick African runners catapulted into strange foreign lands with money in their pockets, alcohol proved to be more of a stubborn opponent and one that refused to be shaken off.

"He was seriously ill about 2001 and was really on his deathbed then," said his agent, Zane Branson, who spread news of Benson's death in September 2003. "He seemed to have recovered somewhat and regained enough health to start doing some running until he fell back into ill-health. Benson was kicking the alcohol when I last saw him, he was dry. He had run the Erewash 10 and failed to break 50 minutes. While that slow time was a surprise to some, Benson and I knew that it was a positive result. He was training properly and with a little more training his times would soon come down again.

"He flew out to Sweden to train with some friends but on returning was denied entry back into England and, after a brief stay in a detention centre near Oxford, was deported to Kenya. Benson's pride found this hard to take and he slipped into depression in Kenya and we soon lost touch."

Fittingly in his last year, he was with his wife Joanne and his two sons. His cousin Cosmas Ndeti, the three-time Boston Marathon champion who Masya introduced to marathon running, and four-time Honolulu champion, Jimmy Muindi, made his funeral arrangements in Kitui, Kenya. Who was to know, watching him win the BUPA Great North Run of 1996, that this would be his ultimate fate?

Thursday, 3rd January 2002

It's cold, wet and miserable outside. Christmas and New Year have been wonderful, but now reality sinks in and I have to go out there and start training for the "Great North Run". I manage four miles, tired, wet and wondering why?

Sunday 6th October 2002

It's the day of the race. With 47,000 runners, this year's race breaks all records. I am running on behalf of Leukaemia research as part of the TV Times team.

Here's the deal: My work colleagues have sponsored me for over £100, providing that I finish the race in less than two hours, on the official race clock. If I fail, I pay double the amount myself.

It's 9 am, just ninety minutes to go before the start. Wrapped in a black bin liner (standard runners' pre-race clothing), I catch a taxi from my hotel in Newcastle up to the start line. The taxi drops me about a mile away, that's as close as you can get. What's an extra mile!

I have planned to meet a couple of mates on the start line by the 1 hour 50 minute marker – they break the start line up into expected finish times to keep the faster runners to the front – so I casually jog up to the top of a grass banking to see where the marker is, only to slip and fall all the way back down! Luckily it's only my pride and shorts that are hurt.

10:30 AM – we're off.

It takes me seven minutes to cross the start line. The weather is perfect, sunny but cool, and the massive crowds really cheer you on. During any long-distance run it helps to tail someone slightly ahead. So I decide to keep pace with two blokes dressed as nuns and two giant bumblebees. Surely they won't beat me?

12 miles on, I am feeling tired and not confident of breaking two hours. The good news is, I left the nuns behind about a mile ago, the bad news is the bumblebees are 100 yards in front and cruising. At last I reach the seafront and the finish line is just in sight. The commentator announces, "Come on, just 70 seconds to go to break two hours" – it's time to sprint!

Now this is quite tough, firstly because it's very crowded and secondly my legs are not very keen on the idea. I sprint across the finish line. 1 hour, 59 minutes and 28 seconds; I've done it.

I came 8,904th, just a couple of places behind the two giant bumblebees.

*Stephen Rosenberg
41, Business Director, Marlborough*

114 Warming to the occasion – insulation blankets: part comfort, part trophy.

1997

ON Sunday August 31, Princess Diana died. It was exactly two weeks before the BUPA Great North Run was to be run, and the organisers were, once again, left with a dilemma.

The nation was in the middle of some of the greatest outpourings of grief it had ever known. Would it be right, or sympathetic to the mood of the people, to stage an event where the background was so traditionally one of smiles and happiness? During the following week, Brendan Foster and the team discussed the options they were faced with and with the race being staged a week after her funeral, the decision was made to go ahead with it.

Of course, had the Run been on September 7th instead of a week later, it might have been different. It would have been staged the day after her funeral and perhaps too close to the emotion of it all. In the end a minute's silence was held before the race and Diana became a theme for many who were running. They had her name on their T-shirts and singlets and Londoner Harmander Singh even carried a Union Flag with the words 'Diana' written across it.

Equally poignantly, despite Princess Diana's tragic early death, the focus of the run – a moment of personal giving – shone through. While the talk of the time was of Diana's death, many of the runners were once again running for the sake of a charity, or in memory of someone they loved. To this day, when 'Abide With Me' is played just before the race, it demonstrates the giving that is such a hallmark of this occasion.

It had been a strange start to the promotion of the Run in 1997 when Foster attended a press conference at the Newcastle Falcons rugby club's home ground at Kingston Park to launch the race. The guest of honour was one of the club's newest signings, the legendary New Zealander Inga Tuigamala. He wore a BUPA Great North Run shirt and sat next to Foster.

As the pair were chatting, Foster told Tuigamala how the idea for the Run had sprung from the time that he had competed in the Round The Bays Race in Auckland, New Zealand, in 1980. Incredibly, Tuigamala, the All Black who had gone on to become one of the best wingers in the world, had actually run in that same race that very year. He was ten years old!

By now, the problems of the mid-1990s were over and the race numbers were increasing again. In 1997, the organisers accepted 36,135 entries, which was up on the previous year by 3683, and on the day of the Run itself, the 'no-shows' were down by 2.2 per cent. There was a new aspect to the entry list too; although it was another entry record for the Run, only 13,500 were from the North East. Here was the confirmation of how the Run had gripped the country.

The race was started by the area's biggest sporting name, Alan Shearer, who flew in by helicopter. The Newcastle striker had a leg in plaster because of an injury but he proved as popular here as he was when leading the line at St James' Park.

But one man began before the others. Sir Jimmy Savile was recovering from a heart operation, but he was determined to make his annual pilgrimage to the North East. He could not run this time – and started ahead of the main event to ensure he could walk the course and still be part of the great occasion.

I ran the Great North Run in 1999. My girlfriend Ann was waiting at 11.5 miles to cheer me on. Unknown to her, I ran with a single red rose and engagement ring and on meeting her I went down on bended knee and asked her to marry me. I am delighted to say she said yes and I think I flew the last 1.5 miles to the finish.

We were married the next year, and now my wife is waiting to greet me at 11.5 miles every time I run the Great North Run. I have run in some exotic places but no race holds such special memories as the Great North Run.

David Smith
36, Pharmacist, Chesterfield

Diabetes UK has been involved in the Great North Run for 25 years and began to recruit runners way back in 1985. Our dedicated runners have raised approximately £330,000 for vital research, which has made a real difference to people with diabetes across the whole of the UK. Many of our runners have inspirational or moving stories to tell.

One of these runners is Mary Jenkins. Mary has had diabetes for 39 years and has been a keen runner since 1988. Unfortunately, since 1990 onwards, Mary has suffered increasing problems with her diabetes which made running very difficult and she had to give up. As the problems escalated her consultant suggested she underwent a revolutionary transplant which could potentially 'cure' her diabetes.

The operation involved the transplantation of insulin-producing islet cells from a donor into Mary's liver. The transplant has meant that she has dramatically reduced her need for insulin injections and has been able to resume running again.

A matter of months after the transplant, Mary decided to run the 2004 Great North Run in aid of Diabetes UK. Mary ran the course in 2 hrs 34 mins and raised £600. Over the years she has raised thousands for Diabetes UK and other charities.

Duncan Roberts
Regional Fundraiser, Diabetes UK Northern and Yorkshire

116, 117 Matching strides. Many run, or should that be take part? Whatever the character displayed is a marvel to behold.

I am just an average runner. My best Great North Run time is 1:34, and worst is 2:20. But the Run has motivated me to keep fit for work and family... it's helped me to be fit enough for living life to the full, and for trying to help others by running for charities like Kidney Research and Leukaemia Research and to raise funds for a laser to treat birthmarks. The first year I ran, my younger daughter was born with a birthmark. My family always turn out to see me at the 5-mile mark, at the Black Bull at Wardley... and what a sight I must be, knee bandages and all!

I haven't got a special story, just the sheer enjoyment of all 24 Great North Runs and the sense of achievement that brings. I'd recommend the experience to anyone and will never forget the thrill of running in Geordieland.

Gordon Booth
58, Pensions Manager, Gateshead

118, 119 Eyes down. Cheeky Sarah catches more than her fair share of passing glances!

Obviously I am biased, but I regard the first Great North Run to have been the most atmospheric. Then again, being only twelve at the time, the event was bound to have had a long-lasting impact on my memory. I had never seen so many people in one place, but my memories of that first Great North Run start before the day of the event.

All the other 23 runs merge into one but I have distinct memories of the first. The cries of, "Oggie! Oggie! Oggie!" echoing around the underpass at the start, the depth of the crowd on the Tyne Bridge and shouts of encouragement all the way. Near the 11 mile mark, when your legs feel tired and the road goes uphill, there was a Clergyman and his congregation cheering away outside their church.

That day the Great North Run brought a Tour De France atmosphere to Tyneside with an enthusiastic crowd that wouldn't allow you to slow in that long last mile.

My whole family took part in that first run, even my parents who were armchair sports fans. Twenty-five years later my sister and I still run and my Mum and Dad cycle to keep fit. To me the Great North Run isn't just about the day of the event it's about the infectious enthusiasm that coaxed the North East up off their armchairs and out running.

Karen Scott
36, Police Officer, Cockermouth, Cumbria

1998

A victory for Sonia O'Sullivan in the elite women's race on her debut in the half-marathon and in the men's, a triumph for Josiah Thugwane, the extraordinary South African who had won the Olympic marathon title in Atlanta two years previously – just a matter of months after he had been shot in the face during a carjacking.

The BUPA Great North Run again broke new ground as police allowed the entries to pass 40,000, and that is exactly what they did: 41,113 signed up for the race, a new record, and there were 29,613 finishers. Impressive figures, and four years on from when the race had its highest amount of 'no-shows' there were now almost 10,000 more finishers than there were then.

It also meant a number of changes in how the race was staged. The date had been put back to October 4th, very much based on the length of the international athletics calendar. It was a year where the European Championships in the summer in Budapest were followed by both the World Cup of athletics in Johannesburg and the Commonwealth Games in Kuala Lumpur in September.

The race's growth was evidence of a second running boom in Britain. Events, now more than just races, such as the Flora London Marathon and the BUPA Great North Run, had produced such startling stories and provided such captivating pictures that those who were there wanted to come back and people viewing from the outside wanted to be part of the action.

By now, it was impossible to find a hotel room from Darlington and Durham to Alnwick in North Northumberland on Great North Run weekend. As Foster said in *The Journal* newspaper: 'We have 20,000 runners coming to the region and those 20,000 will probably bring as many with them again. When you think about the Great North Run, you think about people running down the road, you don't think of it as a huge tourist event.'

But that is what it became. There were runners from 25 different countries competing and again the whole atmosphere was more than just a Run.

This year, Status Quo played at the beginning of the race, which was started by Frank Williams, the Formula One team boss, who was born in the North East. Sir Jimmy Savile was back, running this time after his walk of the year before, along with Paul Burrell, Princes Diana's former butler.

The large numbers meant even greater problems at the finish because of the increase in traffic. Less than two weeks later, the rumour mill was working at full throttle again. This time there were claims that because of the size of the Run, the finish might move to Wearside. Foster was looking towards the Millennium race in 2000, where an even greater number of entrants was expected. Would a new location for the finish improve the race?

Sunderland football club's new ground, the Stadium of Light, or even their old home, Roker Park, were options, and Foster said: "We have to question whether the event is becoming too big for the transport system, especially in South Shields. When you have run 13.1 miles, picked up your medal and your T-shirt... you don't want to take another two hours to get home."

Discussions were held and though the possibility was not ruled out, Foster knew that the seaside location of the finish of the race had been an important factor in why he had wanted to stage the Run in the first place. Many will tell you that the last stretch of coastal road to the end is much longer than they imagined, while others will regale you with tales of how fantastic it is to drop down the hill towards such a picturesque last mile.

South Shields it remained.

opposite Katy Melling/Kevin Gibson

119

John Williamson

Kevin Gibson
opposite: Ad Infinitum

1999

NOT since 1988 had the race been staged in the morning, but the early start time of the race, and its format as the BUPA Great North Run we know today, was established this year. It was not planned. If anything, it happened by chance, but a combination of events now provides the occasion with an even larger identity. It was 40 years since the launch of Grandstand, the BBC's flagship sports show, and, as part of the celebrations, they were broadcasting live from Ascot races, which had been the site of one of their original outside broadcasts.

A host of names, past and present, were there to attend a party. Brendan Foster was invited, as one of the corporation's main, and longest serving, commentators, and during the day he was chatting with Peter Salmon, the then controller of BBC1, and Dave Gordon, the editor of Grandstand.

Gordon says: "We had this conversation about whether it would be a good idea to move the Run to a Sunday morning, have it as a big, standalone programme and start to make more of the event. Peter already had the London Marathon as a morning event, which was successful.

"In 1999, we put more resources into the Run and it has grown from strength to strength. In partnership with the organisers, we have slightly changed the tone of the coverage. We recognise it is not only the elite races that are important but what happens afterwards, because there are tens of thousands running for charities. We have increased the coverage from around two hours to four hours and we treat it as if everyone has a story to tell.

"We work with the organisers to try to identify these human interest stories. Now we have text messaging on screen and even after the elite races have finished, the audience stays at a couple of million which is great for a Sunday morning."

In 1999, the Run started with the wheelchair race at 9.40 am, the women's race five minutes later, and the main field at 10.10 am. That afternoon, England had arranged a friendly football international with Belgium at Sunderland's Stadium of Light. Having the Great North Run in the morning was obviously a perfect way to start what was – and still remains – arguably the North East's biggest sporting day.

The intervention of the BBC provided the race with a greater profile but there was sadness too. Earlier in the year, their sports presenter Helen Rollason had died of cancer and colleagues were running as a tribute to her.

Sally Gunnell, the 1992 Olympic 400 metres hurdles champion, and trackside interviewer, was one of those who swapped her 'working' duties for the day to run. She said: "I got to know Helen at events all over the world and I wanted to do this for her." She was joined by fellow presenters Steve Rider and Ray Stubbs.

While the men's race was won by Kenyan John Mutai, it was those who finished third and fourth in the women's race who would have great significance both then and in the years to come.

Third was Paula Radcliffe, who would become a dominant force at the distance. It was her debut at the half-marathon distance and she ran the second fastest time by a British woman of 69:37. Only Liz McColgan had run quicker. In fourth was Sonia O'Sullivan – competing only 10 weeks after giving birth to her first child.

By now, the extent of outside help was growing. First aid people from Derby, Hull and even Edinburgh were there to help on the day, while this year, at the start, there could not have been a more local flavour to lift the runners than Jimmy Nail, one of the North East's leading rockers, who played before the Run began.

The sun shone and the occasion was summed up by Alan Bell, one of the official starters.

"This event has become an institution. There are many Geordies living abroad who come back specifically to take part. That tells you something about the way people feel about the Great North Run."

MARK LAWRENSON

my part in it...

Former Liverpool and Republic of Ireland defender, turned BBC Television's Match of the Day professional pundit.

I really didn't want to run – why should I? Well sadly a reason came along I never wanted but it made me decide to take part in the Great North Run. My sister passed away three weeks before the run and when Lisa died of breast cancer aged just 45 I thought, 'Well, I've just got to do it'.

But don't get me wrong – I wasn't fit and although I'm a sportsman I was a sprinter, not a long distance runner. But I thought, 'Hey, I'll do it even if I'm not fit for the distance.' I'd done no training but I thought: 'Why not?' And you know what – it was hell.

I think I did it in something like 2.20 in the end but I was all over the place. I was desperate for a pee at four miles. I had to do a Paula (an official pit stop made by a truly great athlete and now used by all-comers who need to go at short notice). Anyway I didn't want to let it go really publicly and there it was – the Esso garage – I pulled over and instead of filling up I let it all go.

That was great but shortly after that at six miles I hit the wall – and a gorilla loped by. I was in bits but I kept going – the crowds were great . Then I got cramp in the thigh of all places at about 10 miles, but then these ladies helped me. They lived in the houses nearby and they gave me some custard creams. It might not be in the official training manual – but it was the drug I needed!

I'd turned up in my trainers and kit – it was really tough but I did it.

Kevin Gibson

1992

Her Majesty the Queen declared 1992 to be her personal annus horribilis as the House of Windsor was rent by a long litany of domestic crises. Princess Anne divorced her husband Mark Phillips, Prince Andrew separated from his wife Sarah 'Fergie' Ferguson and rumours that all was not well even with the Prince and Princess of Wales were fuelled by the publication of Andrew Morton's biography entitled Diana - Her True Story. The Royals were not the only family to find 1992 a difficult year. In September, many homeowners suddenly found themselves saddled with 'negative equity', the situation whereby homes became worth less than their mortgaged value. The crisis was a direct result of the increase in interest rates, which soared to 15% in an attempt to protect the pound's position in the ERM. By the end of the month, sterling's place in a financial mechanism that was supposed, ironically, to prevent wild fluctuations in a currency's value, became completely untenable and Chancellor Norman Lamont took sterling out of the ERM.

123 The Great North Run weekend has world class mile races and numerous other events. CBBC and the BBC coverage of the Great North Run itself ensures that presenters, technicians and the whole team have to be at their best. Meanwhile, fairytales of a different type are being acted out in South Shields.

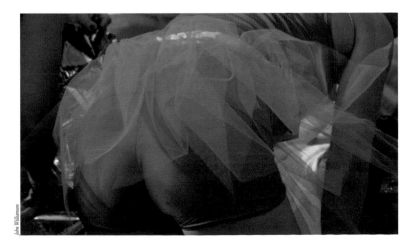

2000

THE BUPA Great North Run had never been staged so late in the year – October 22nd. There was a good reason. The Olympic Games in Sydney was *the* event of the year and did not start until the middle of September.

There was no point in staging the Run beforehand because none of the major elite names would be present. It had become such an established finale to the season that it would be foolhardy to change a winning formula.

Sunday October 1, was the final day of the Olympic Games and one of the main events was the men's marathon, which, in a manner resembling the Great North Run, would include the crossing of a bridge – the Sydney Harbour Bridge, one of the world's most recognised landmarks.

Sonia O'Sullivan, the Great North Run's former winner, was asked by the BBC if she could feature in an advert to promote that year's race and they

Katy Melling

Having seen my brother and father run the Great North Run one year, I decided to take up the challenge. I began dieting and started off tentatively running a few hundred yards. I gradually built this up with the encouragement of my father, which culminated in my running my first ever GNR in 1998. Having lost four stone in weight during this process – I was hooked. Sadly my father passed away from a heart attack, but we buried him with his running kit and much-prized GNR trophies. I have run the GNR every year since 1998 in his memory. Occasionally joined by my elder brother, we have raised money for the British Heart Foundation on each run.

Simon Sturgess
31, Nurse, Soulbury, Bedfordshire

124 Road runner or Emu? Or Greater Tit perhaps! Whichever, a well-earned burger and massage are thoroughly deserved.

Michael Steele/Getty Images
opposite: Ad Hofmann

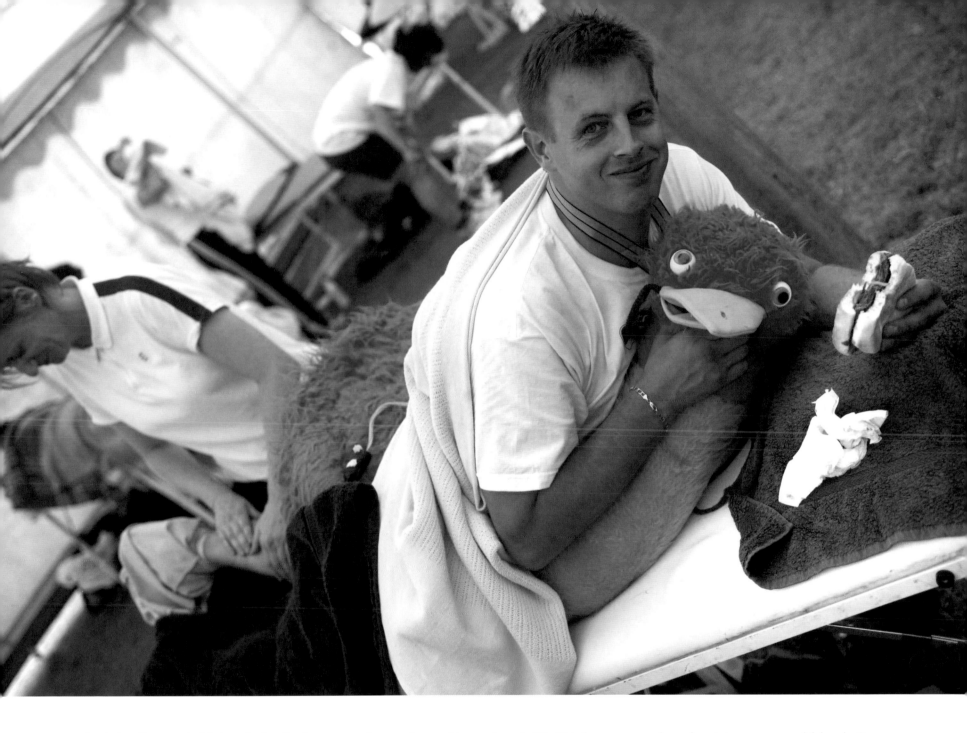

decided to film it on the Harbour Bridge. But how could they shut the bridge to do that? John Caine and Nova's Events Director, David Hart, had a problem to solve.

They spoke to the Olympic and Sydney authorities and it was agreed they could do their filming on the morning of the men's marathon. It was not as straightforward as it sounds. Hart explains: "The bridge was shut for only a specific amount of time as the runners in the marathon were coming towards it. We had this slot where we had to film, and then be off quickly to clear the way so that

the marathon could come through. We did it, but it could have become a bit tricky if more retakes were needed because there would have been nothing we could have done about it."

With The Great North Run being the first race of the new millennium, the Run organisers were allowed to break the 50,000 barrier, with 50,173 entries accepted, and a record 36,822 finishing.

Paula Radcliffe dominated the women's race to win, just weeks after her disappointment in Sydney where she had finished fourth in the 10,000m after dominating the event. It could not

make up for missing out on a medal, but the Run was the start of the healing process.

She had broken the course record and European and British records and she said something which now has incredible resonance: "It shows what I can do on the road. I don't know how good I will be at the marathon and I only hope I can transform this sort of performance into that distance."

Prophetic words indeed.

2001

THE BUPA Great North Run was staged on Sunday September 16th, five days after events took place which changed the world. The 9/11 attacks on the World Trade Centre in New York prompted the organisers of the race to contemplate cancelling their event.

Brendan Foster says: "If it had been a small event, only for local people, we would still have thought twice about staging it. We did not want to be seen as though we were just carrying on as normal.

"Our Run was a national event. And it was the first such occasion to happen after 9/11 – as such, what we did would be remembered. It was something that we had to approach cautiously and correctly."

An event the size of the Great North Run has contingency plans should the race need to be cancelled. The organizers considered their options, one of which was to put it back to the 'secondary' date that they always have should circumstances arise. They spoke with the BBC and with BUPA and the decision was taken to carry on. It became one of the most poignant stagings of the race ever.

The Bishop of Durham was invited to the race. He said a prayer at the start, and beforehand a two minute silence was held. Foster will never forget what happened next, as the BBC cameras panned along the start of the Run.

He says: "There was this runner who was competing carrying a USA flag. It was held up in the crowd as the silence was taking place. It captured the whole mood."

The Run began, and the uplifting spirit of the day produced another marvellous occasion for charities, with around £8 million raised for good causes. Everyone agreed that the decision to stage the event had been the right one.

But 2001 was about more than just the Great North Run and the spin-off races that were being staged nationally. The talk in the aftermath of the Run was about the race's first trip abroad, when it was announced that, in November of that same year, the organisers would be staging the first Great Ethiopian Run.

It has become one of the most inspiring, invigorating and, ultimately, amazing events on the sporting calendar. Here was an event taking place in the land of some of the world's greatest

126, 127 Lest we forget...this poignant flag marked a second of peace in a frenetic day. When "Abide With Me" is played before each start there are few dry eyes. In contrast, even the best need a healthy breakfast.

ever distance runners and with it, an estimated 10,000 Ethiopians took part and 500,000 lined the route of this 10k race.

It started with a request from Myles Wickstead, the British Ambassador to Ethiopia, for a meeting in London to explore the possibility of recreating the BUPA Great North Run on African soil. Fundamental to such a project was a meeting with Haile Gebrselassie, the double Olympic 10,000m champion, and the country's biggest name. Despite all the achievements of his predecessors, Gebrselassie had taken his sport and his country to a new level. He had multiple world records and world titles and has been described as the greatest distance runner in history. His response was instant: total commitment. He wanted an event like this in his homeland. In fact, it had always been his dream.

There were looks of disbelief when Caine said it would become the biggest road running event in Africa, but, in a way not too dissimilar to how the Great North Run had started, everything fitted into place.

Britain's former World Marathon Cup winner Richard Nerurkar had moved to Ethiopia where his wife Gail was undertaking a three-year medical placement as a teaching doctor in Addis Ababa. As events moved on at a quick pace, he willingly became the race director. The British ambassador was a keen jogger and Nerurkar set up his office in the embassy's grounds.

Within weeks the 10,000 entries had been taken up, and on the morning of November 25th it took place. In the central square, the scenes were beyond belief. The noise and the excitement being generated were astonishing. People were watching from every vantage point, from the top of tower blocks to telephone poles.

Gebrselassie was running. But before the start, such was the crush to run, he had to jump on to a podium and ask the crowd to stop, calm down and wait. It was delightful, organised chaos, because the runners of Addis had never seen anything like it and they did not know what to do.

Gebrselassie jumped down from the podium on to the start line, and stumbled just as the race began. Somehow he picked himself up and ran – to win what was such an unbelievable occasion.

The event is now a regular feature on the Great Run calendar. But that first day in Addis, it was something else. Norway's Ingrid Kristiansen, the former marathon world record holder, was one of the special guests. "I have never seen so many people watching one race," she said. A fact you could not dispute.

AT 10.55 am on the day of the 2002 BUPA Great North Run, with thousands of athletes still making their way across the Tyne Bridge, the skies of the North East were treated to another landmark moment in the race. In the distance, first came the noise, and then the aerial acrobats arrived, the magnificent Red Arrows display team, flying above the snake of humanity wending its way to South Shields. Two hours later, they were back performing for the crowds who had gathered by the finish. It was an inspiration for those who were struggling along the coast road to go that extra mile.

Their display brought an end to another superb year for the race; and for one woman in particular. If anyone needed to appreciate what inspiration can be created by the BUPA Great North Run, Jane Tomlinson showed them with a clean pair of heels.

It had been quite a time for Tomlinson. At 38, she had captured the imagination of people outside her native Leeds with the determination she was showing in her fight against cancer.

Tomlinson had run in the Flora London Marathon, she had taken part in a triathlon and entered the BUPA Great North Run having already raised an amazing £50,000 for Cancer Research UK, a figure she aimed to double by running from Newcastle to South Shields. On the morning of the Great North Run she was given support all the way by the cheering crowds, and by her family at the finish of a run which she completed in 1:51.

Tomlinson was 26 when she was diagnosed with breast cancer, and in 2000 she was told it had returned, to her legs and bones, and that she might have only a matter of months to live. She took life by the scruff of the neck, setting herself remarkable challenges at remarkable events. Defying doctor's prognoses, she has now run the Great North on two occasions and her fund-raising exploits have taken the money she has raised to over one million pounds.

128, 129 Pasta, pasta makes us run all the faster – or so they say – but if all else fails, have a piece of choclate cake instead. The pasta party is, to many, the start of the countdown to the run itself.

As she made her way towards the finish, the BBC's television cameras panned in on her; it had been some performance. She had delayed chemotherapy to be part of the Run and she said: "I am so tired and ache everywhere, but it was a fantastic run. The atmosphere was terrific, there's people lining the course all the way and they really are encouraging. I tried hard to get under the 1:55 and I was really struggling at about eight-and-a-half miles, but by eleven-and-a-half I knew I could get there.

"The best parts were the start and the finish, and beating Mike! I feel marvellous. I will keep running but this is my last official event."

It turned out to be anything but.

Brendan Foster summed it up. He said: "Jane and her husband Mike have been an absolute inspiration to everyone associated with this race. Their courage and enthusiasm have touched all of us here today and I am sure all of those watching on television at home."

The people, as usual, never let the race down. Steve Langley, from Sunderland, ran the race with only a leaf to spare his blushes and he told the South Shields Gazette: "I was getting a whole lot of wolf whistles and encouragement along the John Reid Road and the final stretch along the coast was brilliant."

It was estimated that over £8 million was raised for charity. This included the contribution from Mary Laver, a severely disabled woman, who was being pushed in her wheelchair by Yvonne Robb, a deaf nurse. They had met while they were on a trip to Lourdes.

They communicated by having a piece of string tied between them – which either of them would tug if they wanted to stop.

Paul Kosgei, of Kenya, broke the one hour barrier in the men's race, the first time for such an achievement in Britain at the half-marathon.

And then there was Frank Bruno.

He had become a Great North regular, gaining huge support along the way, but it was when the race began that he created the biggest surprise. Never mind Kosgei and company. Bruno charged out from among his fellow celebrities to outsprint the rest of the field and lead the race. It was not long before he was caught, but it was a moment to cherish.

2003

IT was the year of one of the greatest performances in the history of the race, some remarkable stories, tears, cheers and that amazing man in the diver's costume. Paula Radcliffe, Britain's No 1 distance runner, Lloyd Scott, Britain's slowest half-marathoner, and Jim Broadbent, a member of The 146 Club, could not have provided greater contrasts.

There were 35,317 finishers this year with some £10 million raised for charity, a staggering amount on a day when: the runners left 319 bin bags full of clothes on the start line when they set off for South Shields, which the charity SCOPE collected for distribution; Findlays Spring supplied 253,000 bottles of natural spring water for runners; more than 2,500 workers and volunteers assisted on race day; about 18 miles of cloth was distributed and used to make the souvenir T-shirts for the

race; and the Great North Pasta Party, which is held on the night before the race, served up 14,000 portions of fresh pasta and has entered the Guinness Book of World Records for being the world's biggest ever pasta party.

In this year, Radcliffe ran the fastest ever half-marathon by a woman when she won in 1:05:40 while Scott became the slowest finisher in the history of the Great North Run. Wearing his infamous deep-sea diving suit, he completed the course in 31 hours, 44 minutes and 55 seconds. It was a stunning performance from Radcliffe, but unfortunately the record could not be ratified because of the gradients in the course.

Radcliffe broke endless stage records during the run in which she was simply extraordinary. It was a sublime piece of running. In contrast, Scott brought the Run to a close when he slowly made it across the line in his deep-sea diver's gear.

Scott, a former firefighter and professional footballer, competed in the suit, as he had done at the Flora London Marathon where it took him almost a week to complete the course, to raise

I remember the first time I did the GNR. On the way up, the evening before, I started chatting to two other GNR virgins and we all realised that we were actually feeling quite nervous. The next day the feeling persisted, especially when we started walking to the start and saw the masses of people. However, this suddenly evaporated when we saw what can only be described as a very large and overweight 'Hells Angel' with a number proudly pinned on the farthest part of an extremely generous stomach.

All of a sudden we realised what a great event we were in and it didn't matter in the slightest how you got round, it was the taking part that counted.

I've now run five GNRs and am looking forward to carrying on as long as I can put one foot in front of another, and continue to raise money for charity. I've managed to raise £7,500 so far.

I still think of that 'Hells Angel' every year and wonder if he's still running.

Peter Bedwell
48, Financial Advisor, Wakefield

130

opposite: Michael Steele
Kevin Gibson

Kevin Gibson

130, 131 *Taking the plunge – well that's what it's all about – not just talking about it but running – whatever you wear, however long it takes.*

awareness and money for the charity Children with Leukaemia. In the 19 years since he was first diagnosed with the disease, Scott, 43, has raised £4 million.

"The Great North Run was a fantastic experience," he says. "The noise and the support I received was amazing – not that I could hear it all under that helmet. It is heavy and I had to stop all the time because of the weight of the whole costume."

Since 1988, the charity has made grants of nearly £26 million to support research and welfare projects around the country. Scott adds: "It awards grants to areas such as research for causes of Leukaemia, which is unusual because most of it is for the treatment side. But it does also fund pioneering research into treatment.

"It builds specialist units and wards for children to get the best attention and it has premises where children and families can stay to take the stress out of travelling."

Scott will be back in 2005 – but he has been told that he has to finish in daylight hours! He

has swapped the diver's costume for that of a spaceman, and he will be bouncing around the course on stilts!

Stories such as these show how the event still reaches out to people; for those who have taken part in all of them, it can bring both joy and tears.

Jim Broadbent, 57, of Low Fell, experienced both emotions in 2003.

He said: "My friend, Peter Hearn, died suddenly a short while before the race. I asked for his name to be announced on the day and it was really moving. He had done the London Marathon that year, we used to run the Great North together and I had got Peter into the sport years before. He had done the majority of the Great North Runs. It was such a shock, it was devastating.

"When they showed the race on television, you heard his name in the background. I thought about him all of the way through the race. But my daughter Caroline ran in that same race, so there was another emotion. Happiness and sadness in one event."

2004

THE man who raised £10,000 for charity at the BUPA Great North Run of 2004 is a runner who would never describe himself as courageous. He thinks of himself as an ordinary person who has landed in an unfortunate situation. But that is typical of the way Findlay Young talks.

By the time his helicopter flew into the start of the 2004 race Young was preparing for his fourth half-marathon in under 24 hours. He achieved the feat in South Shields and when he crossed the finishing line, he says, quite simply, it was: "Perfect, just perfect."

Perfect indeed and an amazing test of endurance, another remarkable story to add to the thousands, written and unwritten, that have been generated by 24 years of the race that has raised millions for charity. Young is a management consultant who is based in London. Such was the publicity surrounding his efforts that a BBC television crew followed him all the way, featuring him during their coverage of the race.

"I was surprised how the publicity snowballed," he says. "After the race, there was hardly a day when I did not have someone come up to me, either in person or on the telephone, to talk to me about it."

Young is a tremendous character. But his life changed in July 2003 when he was diagnosed as suffering from thyroid cancer. He says: "I had been aware that something was not quite right for a few months prior to that but we did not know what. I had treatment in August and September and I was given the all-clear on September 26." That was the day of that year's BUPA Great North Run.

But Young wanted to do more. He was a runner anyway, ironically running for Cancer Research UK. He had completed the New York and London marathons and had run the Himalayan 100 miles event. It was during training for the Chicago marathon that he was taken ill. He also wanted to run near where he originated from in Castle Douglas in Scotland and when he realised the significance of the date of the Great North Run 2004, a year to the day of being given the all clear, he formulated his remarkable plan.

He selected four half-marathons, starting on the Saturday afternoon before the Great North Run with his last being the race itself. It was some task, but the sort of challenge that Young seems to thrive upon.

132, 133 Bearing up, baring all, keeping fit, having a laugh, singing for your supper, you'll see it all and more at the Great North weekend.

"I started at 1.30 pm. I was in Belfast International Airport. I ran around some of the lakes, and the rural roads around there. It was very scenic, traffic-free. It was a sunny day and I felt strong all the way through and I finished it in just under the two hour mark. The local council and the public relations people at the airport worked out the course for me, and my support crew checked it the day before. We deliberately finished at the airport. We had a quick half an hour to eat and to get some water back inside me before flying to Prestwick Airport (in Scotland) on a small aeroplane. We left the airport at 5.30 pm and drove to Mossdale where the race was starting. There had not been much time to rest but I was feeling fine.

"I ran on the roads I had cycled and driven down tens of thousand of times. They are very rural, and every time I came to a farm or house, there were Cancer Research UK flags there and mile markers and loads of people wishing me well. We finished at Castle Douglas where there were about 100

people: my parents, grandparents, cousins, aunties, lots of school friends.

"We then left at 11.30 pm and flew to Liverpool for our next leg. We landed at 12.30 am and drove to Rhyl in Wales. But when we reached it at 1.30 am we saw the route and decided it could be problematic. It was dark and a bit uneven. We used the standby plan I had at all the places – a treadmill. That was tough, doing a half-marathon through the night on a treadmill, watching the miles tick by.

"But I got through, in 2:15, and there was just one leg to go. By that stage I was feeling weary and hungry but there was no way I was going to give in. We drove back to Liverpool to fly to Newcastle, arriving at 8.30 am. A helicopter took us across to the Great North Run. We flew over the start with 49,000 runners beneath us.

"I was given a place with the elite runners. But the race was still an hour away. At 9.50, I

thought back 12 months. It had been some year. Then the race began. It was tough but the people on the route were so encouraging. With two miles to go, I saw Louise Holland from Cancer UK and I ran past her with the finishing line drawing nearer. I made it. I had achieved my goal."

But his story was not over. In 2005, he ran the Great Manchester Run where he unfortunately revealed that the next day he would be going back into hospital because his cancer had returned.

Mention 2004 to most people connected to BUPA Great North and they will have heard of Findlay Young. He encapsulated everything Brendan Foster had dreamed his race should be. He is one of hundreds of thousands who have run for fun, for the challenge, for loved ones and to raise a few quid (and then some), but his story is also an apt realisation that one man's dream, and many people's hard work and understanding can become everyone's reality and lasting achievement.

133

KELLY HOLMES *my part in it...*

Recently made a Dame as a result of her sublime running culminating in her winning double Gold in the Olympics 2004.

It was brilliant to be there. When you see it on television the atmosphere does not always come across. But when you are there, it's crazy. We were right in the middle and the runners were coming from either side. Everyone was cheering. I hand-slapped 10,000 people probably and they were all telling me 'brilliant'. It really is such a great run. It has grown in such a way. I had run in the Great North Mile the day before, my last race of the season and the first back in Britain after Athens. I like the course of that race. It was so

amazing, so many people came out and there were so many watching me when I was warming up that there were security guards there! The whole weekend is about families, running and fitness. Would I run in it? When I do put my feet up, you want to get me running a half-marathon!?; but I will never say never. Maybe in 2006 they might convince me!

Kelly Holmes, Britain's double Olympic track champion who started the 2004 race.

Finale

THE calm of a November morning by the coast in South Shields. Waves hitting the rocks, a few boats on the horizon, the morning ferry from Holland heading towards Tynemouth.

It is cold, only a handful of people can be seen, and every now and then a car passes by on its way to Sunderland. Can this really be the place that one day each year buzzes with the activity of over 100,000 people?

We know it is because the BUPA Great North Run has caught the imagination of the running public and far beyond. What we are witnessing here this morning is the amazing contrast. How can such a quiet environment become such a fanfare of celebration? It does because of something spectacular – the Great North Run.

Our story has shown how an amazing combination of events brought together a Run that is ever growing. One of its most recent spin-offs, the Great Manchester 10k, attracted 20,000 entrants this year and, if more people had been allowed, it could double this number.

If Brendan Foster had never been invited to New Zealand in 1980, he might never have seen how a city can embrace a sporting occasion such as the Round The Bays race. But he did, and with it his life sent him in a direction that culminated in the Great North Run, which has a healthy future and could be around for as long as man wants to run.

This is one of Foster's aims. One of his friends told him that it would be fantastic to have three copies, then write his own 'My Part' at the end of each and just leave them in his loft for his grandchildren to find one day. Sometime later, they would be brought into a world of discovery about a Run that has brought together young and old, but with his own special memories as well.

As we know, the Great North Run was never meant to become the size it is now, but the runaway train has just not stopped.

While writing this book, I was asked by a friend, a non-runner, what the attraction is of training every day. Where does it lead? What is the point of jogging? Is it just to stay fit? Why put yourself through all that when riding a bike can take you as far and not be so much of a struggle?

Nova International

John Williamson

Nova International

Jim Gibson

When I replied, he was stunned. I told him about the Great North Run, which he had heard of, but it did not dawn on him how much it actually meant to the jogger seen in the street. That if he runs in Newcastle each year, he might break his best time by a second or two.

The existence of the Great North Run drives people to become better runners. If they finish 12,343rd, it does not matter. They have achieved something special and you cannot ask any more than that. Or perhaps you can. In addition to the personal triumphs there has been tale after tale of fund-raising for charity – another aspect of the run that neither Foster or any of his organising team could possibly have predicted in 1981.

It is why the offspring of the Great North Run, in places such as Portsmouth, Manchester, Ireland and Ethiopia, are sellout occasions. It is why, from the south coast of England to East Africa, the day of each race becomes such a glorious occasion.

The pictures of exhausted runners being helped across the line by others at the end of their Great North Run are not generous acts of sportsmanship, but commonplace occurrences. It is the culmination of a task all runners probably set themselves throughout the year – and however the individual runners are feeling, however low their body threshold has become, it will not be enough to stop them making it home.

The next day probably carries the most suffering – in bed, in pain, with blistered feet. And they will have a bug too – a running bug. Within days, maybe even within hours, many will be back on the roads, counting down to the following year's Great North Run.

It is why so many people come back.

The legacy that Brendan Foster has created is to entice people to take their body to that extra limit, to save that extra second.

But put yourself on that start line, hear the noise of the crowd, feel the excitement, and you will realise why the Great North Run is now more than an institution. For many, it is part of their lives.

136, 139 From South Shields to Addis Ababa and from Newcastle's glittering Quayside brimfull of Junior Great North Runners. The Great North Run has spread across the globe. In Manchester and Portsmouth and Dublin 2005 has seen record numbers of runners as the dream to run is taken across the country and into Africa...where to next?...time will tell.

RESULTS

28 June 1981

AN historic opening for more than one reason. Both winners of the first Great North Run were local runners. Perhaps a fitting conclusion to this North East born and bred event – which had taken off following the promotion of Brendan Foster and the BBC "Look North" team.

Mike McLeod crossed the finishing line of what was supposedly the 'Greatest Fun Run Ever' in a time of 1:03:23, his performance echoing Brendan Foster's pre-race assessment that the front of the field would see some serious competition. By the time McLeod had reached one of the race's landmarks, the Tyne Bridge, the race seemed all but over with McLeod ahead, metres ahead and steadily pulling away. Øyvind Dahl tried in vain to match the impressive pace of the Elswick Harrier but in the end had to settle for a race-long battle with Mike Kearns.

At a more steady pace, Foster and a very young Steve Cram jogged home comfortably, with Kevin Keegan, then Captain of the England football team, given an immense cheer from the crowds lining the route as he completed the course.

Karen Goldhawk, back home on her sand-dancer soil, went into the history books as the first women's champion, her time of 1:17:36 being a very respectable clocking for a club runner.

Men's	1st Mike McLeod	1:03:23
	2nd Øyvind Dahl (NOR)	1:04:34
	3rd Mike Kearns	1:04:39
Women's	1st Karen Goldhawk	1:17:36
	2nd Margaret Lockley	1:20:36
	3rd Mary Chambers	1:26:24
Wheelchair	Alan Robinson	1:28:54

26 June 1982

THE following June, it was pretty much the same in the men's race with McLeod retaining his title. The future Olympic 10,000 metres silver medallist won in 1:02:44. He had another impressive win ahead of a strong run from Kevin Forster in the North East drizzle. Half an hour later the light rain turned to a downpour. Undeterred, thousands of spectators at South Shields cheered home the 20,500 competitors. The rain was torrential, bouncing off the South Shields tarmac. Despite this, not a soul in the crowd sought refuge. As the field splashed to the finish, so the crowd cheered, soaked to the skin. Everybody revelled in the occasion. Unlike the previous year, McLeod delayed his move until the coast road where he opened a 14 second winning margin. Margaret Lockley, who had travelled from the Isle of Man for the race, won in impressive style, recording a time of 1:19:24.

Men's	1st Mike McLeod	1:02:44
	2nd Kevin Forster	1:02:58
	3rd Ian Gilmour	1:03:11
Women's	1st Margaret Lockley	1:19:24
	2nd Maureen Hurst	1:20:48
	3rd Sheila Glass	1:21:55
Wheelchair	Alan Robinson	1:32:00

Mike McLeod

Margaret Lockley

19 June 1983

THE reputation of the Great North Run was expanded massively in 1983 when Olympic 10,000m silver medallist and 1984 Marathon gold medallist Carlos Lopes made the trip from Portugal to take the title. As good as the performance was by the athlete who took Gold at the Olympics the following year, Lopes missed McLeod's course record by two seconds. The North East was enjoying its first hot day of the summer and the Portuguese star revelled in the conditions. Finnish runner Pertii Tiainen tried to stay with him but he was shaken off at the five mile point.

However the women's event saw Julie Barleycorn from Crawley run a memorable time of 1:16:39 for a third British victory in a then course record time. Little did she know it would be another nine years before another domestic runner was crowned champion in the women's event. Barleycorn later became Coleby when she married Course Director, Max Coleby.

Men's	1st Carlos Lopes (POR)	1:02:46
	2nd Ray Smedley	1:04:34
	3rd Tommy Persson (SWE)	1:05:07
Women's	1st Julie Barleycorn	1:16:39
	2nd Maureen Hurst	1:19:07
	3rd Karen Goldhawk	1:21:52
Wheelchair Men's	John Grant	1:17:16
Wheelchair Women's	Maria Dodsworth	2:27:29

17 June 1984

A NORWEGIAN double. The summer prior to the 1984 Olympics saw world champion distance runner, Grete Waitz, arrive at Newcastle airport to foray into battle from the city start to the coastal finish.

Waitz, the pioneer of women's distance running and the reigning world marathon record holder, produced a wonderful showing to score a 1:10:27 success. Completing a great day for Norway, Oyvind Dahl, runner-up behind McLeod in the inaugural race, was crowned men's champion in 1:04:36. Fittingly, the race that year was dubbed 'The Great Norse Run'. The men's race was particularly keenly contested with Dahl, despite several efforts, only managing to throw off the challenge of fellow Scandinavian Pertii Tiainen with a sprint in the last 300 metres.

Waitz's success had been a rout and her official placing was 19th in the whole field – she ran in exactly the same time as Tynedale's Nick Speed, one of the North East's foremost road runners – it was a memorable piece of running from a great athlete.

Men's	1st Øyvind Dahl (NOR)	1:04:36
	2nd Pertti Tiainen (FIN)	1:04:41
	3rd Graham Smith	1:06:44
Women's	1st Grete Waitz (NOR)	1:10:27
	2nd Maureen Hurst	1:16:48
	3rd Lorna Irving	1:17:26
Wheelchair Men's	Terry Clark	1:10:28
Wheelchair Women's	Ellen Hodgson	2:50:42

Carlos Lopes

Øyvind Dahl

30 June 1985

A SIGNIFICANT day for British men's running at the Great North Run – not that anyone realised it at the time. When Salford Harrier Steve Kenyon triumphed in a time which equalled Mike McLeod's course record, the victory was celebrated like that of previous British winners. Incredibly, he is the last British man to win the event.

Since then, the best British athletes – Steve Jones, Eamonn Martin, Richard Nerurkar, Jon Brown, Paul Evans, et al – have tried their hardest but died at the sword of overseas visitors. He described the victory as "very sweet". McLeod himself, defeated for the first time in a half-marathon, finished some 300 metres behind Kenyon.

The brilliant little Portuguese star and European Marathon champion Rosa Mota became the first ever female to smash the 70 minute barrier on British soil for the half-marathon, when motoring down the course in a time of 1:09:54. The reputation of the Great North Run was growing with every year.

"What do I remember most? The support of the vast crowds and the encouragement they offered," said the Portuguese star recalling her first victory. "It made me determined to return in the future and win again. It was a great occasion."

Men's	1st Steve Kenyon	1:02:44
	2nd Mike McLeod	1:03:31
	3rd Bernie Ford	1:04:01
Women's	1st Rosa Mota (POR)	1:09:54
	2nd Ann Ford	1:11:36
	3rd Sarah Rowell	1:13:36
Wheelchair Men's	Mark Tong	1:17:18
Wheelchair Women's	Anne Graham	2:26:53

8 June 1986

STEVE JONES of Britain, former holder of the world best for the marathon, set a UK record of 1:00:59 – but still saw himself outrun by Mike Musyoki, the Olympic 10,000 metres bronze medallist. It was a classic encounter. Jones, who had managed only five weeks of training following an achilles tendon injury had hoped, prior to the race, to clock between 62 and 63 minutes. He held the gap as Musyoki maintained his extraordinary pace but the Kenyan opened up a 30 metre-plus gap on the rise to Wardley and finished in 1:00:43, 12 seconds inside Mark Curp's former world best, which had been set in Philadelphia the previous September.

On a marvellous day for the Run, there was also a UK All-Comers' mark of 1:09:45 from Lisa Martin, of Australia, who took 9 seconds off the UK-All-Comers and course best set by Rosa Mota the previous year.

Men's	1st Mike Musyoki (KEN)	1:00:43
	2nd Steve Jones	1:00:59
	3rd Steve Kenyon	1:01:31
Women's	1st Lisa Martin (AUS)	1:09:45
	2nd Véronique Marot	1:12:06
	3rd Ann Ford	1:12:13
Wheelchair Men's	Chris Hallam	1:01:15
Wheelchair Women's	Karen Davidson	1:13:04

Steve Kenyon

Steve Jones

27 June 1987

LISA MARTIN returned 12 months later, with compatriot and world marathon champion Rob De Castella, and the Aussie pair matched the Norwegian double of Dahl and Waitz in 1984.

But De Castella provoked plenty of controversy.

The World and Commonwealth champion tampered with his number – appropriately 13 – allowing his own sponsor's names to appear as well as that of Pearl Assurance, the official race backers. De Castella had barely crossed the line 24 seconds ahead of Scotland's Allister Hutton in 1:02:04, when taken to task by race referee David Littlewood.

Littlewood initially suspended the superstar who had flown in from Boulder, Colorado, but after an appeal he was reinstated as race winner.

"I always cut my number like that," said De Castella. "It makes it more comfortable and allows more air to circulate around your body which is vital to runners. I thought it was okay as long as the name of the race sponsor wasn't removed. I'll have to be more careful in the future."

The incident was the exception, his victory went like clockwork, and could not detract from a world class performance.

Martin scored a decisive victory ahead of Waitz also breaking away at the 10-Mile marker to win in 1:10:00. Her Scandinavian rival finished 38 seconds in arrears with Veronique Marot claiming third place in 1:11:17.

Men's	1st Rob de Castella (AUS)	1:02:04
	2nd Allister Hutton	1:02:28
	3rd Tony Milovsorov	1:02:30
Women's	1st Lisa Martin (AUS)	1:10:00
	2nd Grete Waitz (NOR)	1:10:38
	3rd Véronique Marot	1:11:17
Wheelchair Men's	Chris Hallam	0:56:37
Wheelchair Women's	Karen Davidson	1:19:55

I did my first run in 1995, and have managed to keep an orange number for almost every year. This was particularly difficult in 1999 as I did the race 10 days after my vasectomy. "Things" were a bit sore but I managed to get around in only a few minutes more than my predicted time by wearing a pair of swimming trunks beneath my shorts to minimise "bounce". My surgeon didn't know whether to be impressed or horrified when I told him!

Geoff Wilson
45, Optometrist, Durham

Rob de Castella

Chris Hallam

24 July 1988

GRETE WAITZ, recovered from a hip injury, returned the following year to produce a memorable performance, a UK All-Comers' record time of 1:08:49. In so doing she slashed 56 seconds from Lisa Martin's previous course record.

Her powerful front running brought out the very best in Susan Tooby who lowered the British record to 1:09:56.

Ireland's John Treacy, the 1984 Olympic marathon silver medallist, scored an untroubled victory, winning the men's race in 1:01:00. Considering this was his road race debut it was quite some performance. He was particularly pleased with the winning time, given the windy conditions experienced in the early stages of the race.

Men's	1st John Treacy (IRL)	1:01:00
	2nd Steve Jones	1:01:58
	3rd Mike O'Reilly	1:02:42
Women's	1st Grete Waitz (NOR)	1:08:49
	2nd Susan Tooby	1:09:56
	3rd Paula Fudge	1:11:37
Wheelchair Men's	David Holding	0:57:57
Wheelchair Women's	Josie Cichockyj	1:37:38

Having run around Newcastle whenever I could, it felt natural that I should do the Great North Run – which I first did in 1989. Whilst training for the 1997 run I was diagnosed with heart problems at 39 – and within eight months had a quadruple heart bypass. The thought of ever running again terrified me – it was all over. But my surgeon was brilliant. He said, 'I want you doing a half-marathon in six months!' It took longer, but with good rehab, and with the confidence that the medical and rehabilitation staff gave me, I realised it was possible. On that wonderful sunny day – with my 'Heart Bypass – Please Pass By' T-shirt on – I ran, and walked, and got to the finish. My heart was fully functioning. There was nothing I couldn't do!

Neil Sutcliffe
46, Accountant, Lancashire

John Treacy

EVEN before Mustapha Ennechchadi won a thrilling photo-finish ahead of Mike McLeod, spectators on the Tyne Bridge had seen Todd Bennett win a high powered 200 metres road race, while the packed crowds at the finish had even more to enthuse over.

John Walker and Steve Ovett fought a battle over the last one mile of the GNR course, the New Zealander winning by half-a-second in a superfast time of 3:53.08.

While they were locked in battle, 1988 Olympic marathon champion Gelindo Bordin was aiming to show his legs could also cope with the much faster half-marathon pace.

They did not, the wheels came off for the Italian in the last mile as Ennechchadi – an unknown Moroccan – and McLeod, the two-times Geordie winner, went into overdrive.

There was nothing to separate the pair at the finish but Ennechchadi got the verdict, although both contestants were given the same time of 1:02:39.

Lisa Martin put in a late surge to win a third title, breaking away from Carla Buerskens to beat the Dutchwoman by five seconds in 1:11:03. "It wasn't too hot out there," insisted Martin the future wife of World 10,000m record holder Yobes Ondieki, of Kenya. "I've just come from Phoenix where it's 109° – so 70° is fine.'

Veronique Marot, despite the relative heat, treated the race as a training session. But her time of 1:12:45 was still good enough for third place.

Men's	**1st** Mustapha Ennechchadi (MAR)	1:02:39
	2nd Mike McLeod	1:02:39
	3rd Gelindo Bordin (ITA)	1:02:49
Women's	**1st** Lisa Martin (AUS)	1:11:03
	2nd Carla Beurskens (NED)	1:11:08
	3rd Véronique Marot	1:12:45
Wheelchair Men's	Chris Hallam	1:01:40
Wheelchair Women's	Eileen Dixon	2:06:54

Mustapha Ennechchadi

Grete Waitz

Lisa Martin

16 September 1990

THERE was a major revamp for the 1990 race, when the decision was taken to move the event out of the track season into autumn. To accommodate TV coverage, the meeting was moved to mid–September, despite clashing with the last major track international of the season in Sheffield.

The decision was justified when, in another thriller, Steve Moneghetti broke the world record. The uncompromising Australian mastered the wily skills of world marathon champion Douglas Wakiihuri, beating off the Japanese-based Kenyan by eight seconds in 1:00:34.

Sadly, the distractions, particularly of Steve Cram and Peter Elliott doing battle over a mile in Sheffield, robbed Moneghetti's achievement of the recognition it fully deserved in the national media.

1988 Olympic Marathon Champion, Rosa Mota, scored her second success at the Great North Run when crossing the finishing line in a very fast time of 1:09:33 – and promptly donated her winner's cheque to the children of a local special school. The cooler conditions had favoured quicker times as the winner said: "I felt cold at the start, so I ran slowly until 5km and then I started to race." Shortly after, the race was effectively over, as she stormed past Carla Beurskens and Grete Waitz who filled the minor places.

Men's	1st Steve Moneghetti (AUS)	1:00:34
	2nd Douglas Wakiihuri (KEN)	1:00:42
	3rd Mark Flint	1:02:10
Women's	1st Rosa Mota (POR)	1:09:33
	2nd Carla Beurskens (NED)	1:10:24
	3rd Grete Waitz (NOR)	1:10:51
Wheelchair Men's	Chris Hallam	0:56:32
Wheelchair Women's	Tanni Grey	1:05:08

A few memories from the Great North Run: From the first few runs with other members of Tynemouth Rowing Club, trying to break the one hour thirty barrier (never quite got there, 1:31 being the fastest I achieved), enjoying the huge crowds while getting to the finish – tired but happy, meeting up with other friends and walking to South Shields seafront and queuing for fish and chips before wading out into the cold sea to be picked up by the Rowing Club rescue boat and thus avoiding the long queues for the ferry. Once back at the Rowing club, having a B.B.Q and a few beers to round off the day.

In 2003 I was wondering how I was going to maintain my 100% record, having ripped my Achilles Tendon in July and still being in plaster at the time of the run. Help was on hand in the form of four runner friends, plus my brother Mike who had hired a wheelchair for the day! I started near the back with crutches also on hand and managed to walk across the start line, 100 metres on the John Reid Road and also hobble across the finish line, completing the course in two and half hours. Funnily enough I wasn't even out of breath by the end of it!

Dave McGuire
47, IT Manager, Tynemouth

Steve Moneghetti

Rosa Mota

15 September 1991

THIS year's race signalled the arrival of Benson Masya, the Kenyan who was to prove himself the world's most consistent half-marathon runner.

In the next six years, the rough looking and tough talking African star would four times become the master of this undulating course.

Unlike De Castella four years earlier, Masya suffered no ill-luck when wearing the unlucky number 13 on the front and back of his racing vest. Masya was reckoned by many to have been included in the race as a pacemaker to assist Moses Tanui to smash Moneghetti's world record but proved everyone wrong. Just 21, Masya, a postal clerk and ex boxer from Nairobi, had been asked to take his more elegant Kenyan compatriot through 10 miles in 47 minutes, the hope being that the one-hour barrier might be bettered for the first time ever.

But Tanui, after a heavy track season where he won the World 10,000m gold medal, was forced out of the race with a hamstring injury in the 11th mile.

That allowed Masya to gradually pull clear of the leading pack of Brits who were chasing his tail and score an easy victory in 1:01:28.

Paul Davies-Hale, who made a cautious start, finished ahead of Nick Adams to clinch second place, 11 seconds down on the winner. The Swansea man finished third in 1:01:53.

Norway's Ingrid Kristiansen won an amazing women's race where local girl Jill Hunter started off like a sprinter before blowing-up after 10 ½ miles. "I couldn't believe it, the pace she went," said Kristiansen. "What's she doing – no one can run that fast and finish a half-marathon."

Hunter, who in the spring set a World 10 miles best time, did finish – third in a time of 1:12:24 – but almost four minutes shy of Kristiansen's world record figure.

"I was hoping to get away and then hang on," said the local lass from Valli Harriers. "But I just didn't know enough about the pace needed. When I saw the time for three miles on the lead car, I knew it was too quick and I knew I would pay later."

Once Hunter had paid her dues for her gallant attempt to smash Kristiansen's world figure, the Norwegian herself went into overdrive. The World marathon and 10,000m record-holder drove hard for the finishing line, breaking the tape in 1:10:57. Hunter, who was passed by Andrea Wallace who clocked 1:11:36, admitted she considered dropping out of the race after only six miles.

Then the loveable Geordie pronounced: "But then I thought that I'd have to jog all the way to the finish anyway, to pick up my clothes and stuff. So I just kept pushing."

Men's	1st Benson Masya (KEN)	1:01:28
	2nd Paul Davies-Hale	1:01:39
	3rd Nigel Adams	1:01:53
Women's	1st Ingrid Kristiansen (NOR)	1:10:57
	2nd Andrea Wallace	1:11:36
	3rd Jill Hunter	1:12:24
Wheelchair Men's	David Holding	0:47:24
Wheelchair Women's	Tanni Grey	1:00:22

Benson Masya

Ingrid Kristiansen

20 September 1992

ALL change. The Great North Run really hit the international map. When the International Amateur Athletics Federation announced the half-marathon would replace its 15K event, some greeted it with a degree of sadness.

But they chose Newcastle as the place to stage the first IAAF/Diet Coke World Half-marathon Championships, which were hailed as a massive success after integrating with the mass participation Great North Run.

How many fun runners can tell their future offspring they ran in a World Championship event? IAAF delegates were amazed when police reported almost 700,000 spectators lining the route.

With 19 men and 16 women's teams comprising 180 elite athletes, the inaugural Championships were deemed a successful investment and venture.

Adding to the glamour of an already ritzy occasion, Benson Masya won the title in a world record time of 1:00:24 – IAAF officials stressing it was achieved over a legally certified course. Second man home was Antonio Silio of Argentina in 1:00:40, and 5 seconds behind him, in third place, was Boay Akonay from Tanzania.

The defending GNR men's champion headed the field as it flew over the Tyne Bridge and even when an inspired Akonay, of Tanzania, opened an 80 metres lead after seven–and–a–half miles he remained confident. "I knew I would win and stuck to my own schedule," said Masya.

Kenya took the team title from the host nation who saw fine runs from seventh placed Dave Lewis, Paul Evans 11th and Carl Thackery 17th, just beating off the challenge of Brazil.

To the delight of British fans, Liz McColgan – despite missing Grete Waitz's course record by just four seconds – bounced back to her brilliant best after a disappointing 1992 Olympic Games.

McColgan was a class act roaring to a time of 1:08:53 and a massive 28 seconds winning margin ahead of Japan's Megumi Fujiwara with Rosanna Munerotto of Italy finishing third in 1:09:38.

"It meant everything for me to come here and win today," said the Scot who realised too late she had been suffering from anaemia in Barcelona when fifth over 10,000m. "The crowd were great, they were shouting for me all the way. It's not often you can win a world title in your own country, so this is great for me."

Japan took the team race, with Britain – McColgan, backed by Andrea Wallace 12th and Suzanne Rigg 31st – finishing runners-up ahead of Romania.

Men's	1st Benson Masya (KEN)	1:00:24
	2nd Antonio Silio (ARG)	1:00:40
	3rd Boay Akonay (TAN)	1:00:45
Women's	1st Liz McColgan	1:08:53
	2nd Megumi Fujiwara (JPN)	1:09:21
	3rd Rosanna Munerotto (ITA)	1:09:38
Wheelchair Men's	David Holding	0:50:21
Wheelchair Women's	Tanni Grey	0:59:21

Benson Masya

Liz McColgan

IT WAS third time lucky for Moses Tanui; he claimed his first GNR title with a superlative run of 1:00:15 – a UK All-Comers' record.

Tanui, who, in his debut did not finish and only took **53rd** spot in the World Championships, denied his arch Kenyan rival Benson Masya the glory of completing a hat-trick.

Indeed it was Masya's turn – he was suffering from a back injury after a car crash – to fail to make the finishing line, ironically pulling out at almost the same spot which saw the demise of Tanui two years earlier.

Despite strong headwinds, having detached himself from the rest of the pack after five miles, Tanui atoned for his previous disappointments.

The conditions would deny Tanui the opportunity of challenging the world record of 59 minutes 47 seconds, achieved six months earlier, but it was still a polished performance.

His winning margin at the finish of the race was a huge 90 seconds as Paul Evans headed off the challenge of third placed Richard Nerurkar who clocked 1:01:53.

Tanui said: "I always said I would come back and avenge my disappointment of 1991. The injury I had last year was not the same, but may have been connected."

Tegla Loroupe was the winner of the women's race in 1:12:55 ahead of 1988 Olympic 10,000m gold medallist Olga Bondarenko, the Russian trailing her by 18 seconds.

But for the crowd it was the presence of the third finisher that occupied most of their attention – and massive support – throughout the length and breadth of the course.

"Howway Zola," was the Geordie cry which heralded the appearance of Zola Pieterse, as she gamely challenged for the coveted GNR title.

The hopes of the former Zola Budd ended in the last mile. But the controversial athlete who was given UK citizenship to compete in the 1984 Olympic Games, returned home to South Africa in a happy frame of mind. "I really felt good until the last mile," said Pieterse, the change in terrain when descending Marsden Bank at 12 miles ending her victory prospects.

Men's	1st Moses Tanui (KEN)	1:00:15
	2nd Paul Evans	1:01:45
	3rd Richard Nerurkar	1:01:53
Women's	1st Tegla Loroupe (KEN)	1:12:55
	2nd Olga Bondarenko (RUS)	1:13:13
	3rd Zola Pieterse (RSA)	1:13:30
Wheelchair Men's	Ivan Newman	0:54:11
Wheelchair Women's	Rose Hill	0:58:00

Moses Tanui

Tegla Loroupe

KENYAN Benson Masya became the first man to win the Great North Run title on three occasions – but it took a photo-finish replay to confirm the result.

In a crowd thriller, Masya ran 1:00:02 – a UK All-Comers' record which would stand for eight years – to beat compatriot Moses Tanui when they battled out their approach to the finishing line.

Tanui, who was judged to be a second adrift of his fellow Kenyan, to this day still queries the result announced after a short delay by the meeting referee.

"I won that race," Tanui said from his home in Eldoret. "Just look at the photographs at the finish – I was the winner."

There was never any love between the two ace athletes – Tanui possessing the refined style of a gentleman while Masya, the ex-boxer, appeared a more rough and ready character.

With Paul Tergat – then just an up-and-coming youngster – a distant third in 1:00:42 it was a clean sweep of the medals for the African nation.

Rosanna Munerotto, World bronze-medallist two years earlier, returned to the race to become Italy's first – and only – champion.

Munerotto, who reckoned her third place in 1992 was the greatest performance of her international career, held off the challenge of Andrea Wallace to win by five seconds in 1:11:29.

Men's	1st Benson Masya (KEN)	1:00:02
	2nd Moses Tanui (KEN)	1:00:03
	3rd Paul Tergat (KEN)	1:00:42
Women's	1st Rosanna Munerotto (ITA)	1:11:29
	2nd Andrea Wallace	1:11:34
	3rd Manuela Machado (POR)	1:11:48
Wheelchair Men's	David Holding	0:50:33
Wheelchair Women's	Rose Hill	1:00:41

1993

The year's box office smash was Schindler's list, Steven Spielberg's film that told the story of the life of an Austrian businessman who saved thousands of Jews during WWII. Shot in black and white, the film graphically recreated the horrors of Nazi concentration camps and if we thought such atrocities belonged to history, the Bosnian Civil War taught us otherwise. The Bosnian War also gave the English language the sinister phrase 'ethnic cleansing' to describe the forced removal of minority groups from their homes. Yet as Bosnians, Serbs and Croatians fought for control of the tiny Adriatic state, peace seemed to be breaking out in other conflicts. International sanctions against South Africa were lifted at the request of Nelson Mandela and the newly-installed US President Clinton presided over a peace accord between Yasser Arafat of the PLO and Israeli Premier Yitzhak Rabin.

Rosanna Munerotto

1994

The much vaunted 'global village' became a reality in 1994 with the public launch of a new computer system named the World Wide Web. The Web was originally created in 1989 by British physicist Tim Berners-Lee, to allow academics to exchange ideas through a system of computers linked over the internet and he gave his system to the world for nothing! Other technological advances announced in 1994 included the first digital video/ versatile disk (DVD) developed in a joint venture by Sony and Phillips and three machines named Arthur, Lancelot and Guinevere. The mythological names were no accident as these curious contraptions were created for Camelot, the company selected to run Britain's first national lottery. Across the Irish Sea even more momentous events were taking place when, after 25 years of 'armed struggle', the Irish Republican Army finally declared "a complete cessation of military activities" in Northern Ireland.

1995

A curiously British scandal broke in January 1995 with the collapse of Barings, Britain's oldest merchant bank. Nick Leeson, a Baring's trader based in Singapore, lost nearly £1 billion on the volatile futures market. Another notable name to cease trading in 1995 was the Today newspaper. Britain's first full colour daily, launched by flamboyant publisher Eddie Shah in 1986, was also the first to use the new technology which finally broke the power of Britain's print unions. Thankfully, the collapse of Barings and Today did not mark a return to the recessionary days of the early eighties; instead the wails of shareholders were drowned by a blizzard of guitar music. Spearheaded by bands such as Blur, Oasis and Pulp, the new Britpop sound seemed to echo the heady days of the swinging sixties and suddenly it was cool to be British once more.

17 September 1995

THREE YEARS after winning the World half-marathon title, Liz McColgan returned to Tyneside determined to kick-start a "new career" with another victory.

"The road is where my career is going now," insisted McColgan whose win clearly showed she was back at her very best after a knee injury had threatened her career. The Scot arrived at the meeting with a new coach – Grete Waitz, the GNR course record-holder who McColgan had admired ever since becoming a distance athlete. McColgan said: "This race was really a learning experience for me because Grete gave me instructions to sit and not make the pace today. I usually go to the front."

But the 31 year old McColgan did take the lead and her telling burst and change of speed after eight miles was matched only by Portugal's world marathon champion Manuela Machado and Fatuma Roba, the Ethiopian who would go on to win the following year's Olympic marathon gold medal.

Machado had again to settle for third position when feeling the strain after nine miles. However Roba pluckily held on until the closing stages, before McColgan pulled away to win in 1:11:42 – an excellent time given the windy conditions.

Roba had the satisfaction of posting a season's best with Machado, who in fairness was still running with the strain of the Gothenburg marathon in her legs, third in 1:13:22.

But it was a day of celebration for the resurrection of McColgan's career and positive proof that her link-up with two-times GNR champion Waitz, could work.

"I'm very pleased for Liz and she ran the race how I wanted her to – she's becoming more obedient," said the Norwegian of her new pupil whose previous coaches had found her a handful to train.

Moses Tanui turned the tables on Benson Masya, and, considering the windy conditions, produced an excellent time of 1:00:39 to regain his GNR title.

It was an authoritative victory by the Kenyan who at the finish held a massive lead of over 80 seconds ahead of his fellow Kenyan, Masya, with another of their countrymen James Kariuki third in 1:02:29.

Nevertheless Tanui's time was the fifth fastest in the world at that stage of the season as he again demonstrated his mammoth ability over what was for him, the perfect distance.

Men's	1st Moses Tanui (KEN)	1:00:39
	2nd Benson Masya (KEN)	1:01:59
	3rd James Kariuki (KEN)	1:02:29
Women's	1st Liz McColgan	1:11:42
	2nd Fatuma Roba (ETH)	1:12:05
	3rd Manuela Machado (POR)	1:13:22
Wheelchair Men's	Jack McKenna	0:52:16
Wheelchair Women's	Tanni Grey	0:58:44

Moses Tanui

Tanni Grey-Thompson

BENSON MASYA returned to score his fourth and final victory – but the Run's most prolific winner made it very apparent that he was competing as a favour to the race organisers.

On race week Thursday, Southport-based Masya was back on Tyneside, supping a pint in local pub the Dolly Peel, and telling local journalists that victory would be his.

Predictably, he proved to be correct – but the win was achieved only after a great battle with Paul Evans, who, sticking like an elastoplast to Masya's back, looked in with a chance of achieving a British win for the first time since Steve Kenyon 11 years earlier.

But it was not to be. After 10 miles, Masya, although not in the best of form, powered away to score what would be his last victory in a race which he said was his "Cup final."

There was drama in the women's race when Liz McColgan looked doomed to lose her previous year's title when trailing Esther Kiplagat with only 400 metres of the race remaining. McColgan had trailed her Kenyan rival by 12 seconds with a mile remaining but she doggedly stuck to the task in hand and, with a wonderful turn of speed, snatched victory.

"When you've fought back from a two-year injury battle and been told you'll never race again, a mere 12-second gap is nothing," said the jubilant Scot after notching her third GNR win.

But it was a closely run affair with McColgan's unmatchable speed allowing her to power past Kiplagat only 200 metres away from The Leas finishing line then open an eight second gap to win in 1:10:28, the runner-up a spent force.

Men's	1st Benson Masya (KEN)	1:01:43
	2nd Paul Evans	1:01:55
	3rd Antonio Serrano (ESP)	1:01:58
Women's	1st Liz McColgan	1:10:28
	2nd Esther Kiplagat (KEN)	1:10:36
	3rd Jane Salumäe (EST)	1:11:54
Wheelchair Men's	David Holding	0:49:17
Wheelchair Women's	Tanni Grey	0:57:17

1996

The fragile IRA ceasefire was broken on February 9th with the explosion of a bomb in London's Docklands. The detonation of half a ton of explosives caused widespread damage to new developments around Canary Wharf and put the Ulster peace process in jeopardy, but terrorism was not suspected to be the cause of a fire in the Channel Tunnel. Miraculously no-one was hurt in the blaze which destroyed a shuttle train and its cargo of lorries but the little town of Dunblane in Central Scotland was not to be so lucky. On March 13th, a psychologically disturbed gunman named Thomas Hamilton shot dead 16 primary school children and their teacher before turning the

gun on himself. In the countryside, the BSE crisis in British farming deepened as a result of a ban on UK beef exports imposed by the European Union. The ban followed the British government's admission that there was an apparent link between BSE in cows and the human brain disorder known as Creutzfeld-Jacob Disease (CJD).

1997

In May's General Election, Tony Blair's modernised 'New Labour' party won a landslide victory that ended 18 years of Conservative supremacy in British politics. The new prime minister's spin doctors and publicists quickly capitalised on the mood of optimism in the country by coining the phrase 'Cool Britannia' to describe Britain's pre-eminence in fashion, music and popular culture. The personifications of Cool Britannia were Posh, Baby, Scary, Sporty and Ginger – better known as The Spice Girls. The chart topping 'girl-power' group was created by pop impresario Simon Fuller and at Edinburgh's Roslin Institute a more controversial exercise in creation was taking place. Deep moral questions were raised by the announcement that British scientists had managed to clone 'Dolly the Sheep'. More questions were asked on August 31st when it was announced that the Princess of Wales had been killed in a car crash. Few people will forget where they were when they heard the dreadful news that Diana's Mercedes had crashed into the concrete wall of a Parisian underpass.

1998

The Northern Ireland peace process, so nearly derailed by the Dockland's bomb, was put back on track with April's Good Friday Agreement between the British and Irish Governments. Amazingly, the Agreement survived Ulster's worst terrorist atrocity to date, the explosion of a car bomb in the market town of Omagh which killed 28 people, including 15 children. Across the Atlantic, US President Clinton found himself embroiled in the Monica Lewinsky scandal after he admitted an 'inappropriate physical relationship' with the young White House intern. Clinton became the first sitting president to face a Grand Jury and only the second to be impeached (Andrew Johnson was the first in 1868 and Nixon resigned before his impeachment for the Watergate scandal began) but he was acquitted and the 'Comeback Kid' remained in the Oval Office. Besides the Lewinsky affair, UK newspaper headlines were dominated by the trial of Louise Woodward, the British nanny accused of shaking to death a toddler while working for a Boston family.

THERE was a shock defeat for Liz McColgan in a race where she was aiming to achieve a record-breaking fourth victory.

McColgan failed to get her tactics right and found herself relegated to third place behind Lucia Subano and Marian Sutton.

The Kenyan won the race in a time of 1:09:24 with Britain's Sutton, who ran brilliantly, finishing in a lifetime best of 1:09:41, while McColgan was third in 1:10:08.

It was her first ever loss in the Tyneside Classic and afterwards she insisted the defeat was down to herself.

McColgan, not wanting to go off too quickly, said: "I held back and held back, but when I started to get my head down it was too late.

"It seems stupid to say, but the half-marathon was just too short for me today. I thought the others would 'die' later in the race, but, unfortunately for me, they didn't."

Sutton, running two minutes faster than ever before, moved to third place on the UK All-Time list with her superb run.

She said: "I knew Lucia was stronger than me and she broke me at 10 miles. That last mile was really tough. I was really determined to be the first British finisher. It's nice to beat Liz, but I know she is a better runner than she showed today."

Once again, there was an expectation that Jon Brown or Paul Evans might clinch a first British victory since Steve Kenyon's 1985 success. But "rookie" half-marathoner Hendrik Ramaala spoiled the party for the British boys winning what was only his second race over the distance.

The South African won in a time of 1:00:25, pulling well clear in the last mile ahead of the chasing pair of Wilson Cheruiyot and Sammy Korir who clocked 1:00:41 and 1:00:43 respectively.

Cheruiyot, who was not among the elite entries for the race, had to pay the the entry fee of £14 to compete, then saw off his more fancied opponents.

Evans, twice a runner-up, clocked a personal best of 1:01:18 for fourth position with Brown, who flew in from Vancouver for the race, sixth in 1:01:49.

Men's	1st Hendrik Ramaala (RSA)	1:00:25
	2nd Wilson Cheruiyot (KEN)	1:00:41
	3rd Sammy Korir (KEN)	1:00:43
Women's	1st Lucia Subano (KEN)	1:09:24
	2nd Marian Sutton	1:09:41
	3rd Liz McColgan	1:10:08
Wheelchair Men's	David Holding	0:44:22
Wheelchair Women's	Tanni Grey	0:52:17

4 October 1998

IRELAND'S Sonia O'Sullivan defied a cruel North Sea wind to make her half-marathon debut in solid style with a superb victory. O'Sullivan crossed the South Shields finishing line with a huge smile on her face in 1:11:50, over a minute ahead of European marathon champion Manuela Machado, of Portugal, with Kenya's Pamela Chepchumba third.

It was a fitting end to the Irishwoman's stunning season – a year in which she had won the World Cross-Country long and short course races, completed a unique European 5,000 metres and 10,000 metres double and won the World Cup 5,000 metres title.

After a fast first mile of 5min 9secs from the start on Newcastle's central motorway, the trio quickly broke away from the remainder of the field.

That proved the easy part for them, but the biting headwind proved a constant obstacle as they attempted to shelter themselves behind one another in the uncomfortable conditions.

The 19 year old Chepchumba was the first to feel the strain, falling back five miles from the finish after Machado put in a punishing burst at the beginning of a steady climb to the South Shields coastline.

O'Sullivan still looked comfortable. She'd done her homework and was prepared for the tactic, knowing this was the spot where Liz McColgan destroyed Machado three years previously when the Portuguese woman eventually placed third.

After the 10 mile marker a telling burst from O'Sullivan quickly took her 20 then 40 yards clear and it was apparent that only a major disaster would prevent the Irish star ending her season on a terrific winning note.

Over the final mile to the finishing line the massive crowd in excess of 20,000 cheered every stride as O'Sullivan won by 65 seconds with Chepchumba a long way behind in 1:14:42.

O'Sullivan said: "It is a great way to end my year. The only thing that spoiled it really was the cold. It was freezing out there and 13 miles is a long way to run. I was running well within my capabilities. My form lived up to expectations and everything went fine."

Atlanta Olympic marathon champion Josiah Thugwane made it a second successive victory for South Africa, flying in from New Mexico and coasting to victory in 1:02:32. Second came John Mutai in 1:02:50, and third was Martin Fiz in 1:03:30.

Men's	1st Josiah Thugwane (RSA)	1:02:32
	2nd John Mutai (KEN)	1:02:50
	3rd Martín Fiz (ESP)	1:03:30
Women's	1st Sonia O'Sullivan (IRL)	1:11:50
	2nd Manuela Machado (POR)	1:12:55
	3rd Pamela Chepchumba (KEN)	1:14:42
Wheelchair Men's	Hadj Lahmar	0:53:47
Wheelchair Women's	Tanni Grey Thompson	1:10:58

Hendrik Ramaala

Lucia Subano

Josiah Thugwane

Sonia O'Sullivan

151

10 October 1999

ALL KENYA this year as John Mutai and Joyce Chepchumba scored a double for their country, winning their respective races in Newcastle in spectacular style.

Mutai, runner-up last year, recorded one of the fastest times in the 19 year history of the event to win the men's race in 1:00:52.

The Midlands-based athlete, who had prepared for the race at altitude, made no mistake after his defeat the previous year.

Already clear in the opening part of the race he went through five miles in 22:49, with South Africa's Gert Thys leading the chase but 100 metres in arrears.

A 4:26 split for the seventh mile saw Mutai still in a commanding lead and although Thys narrowed the gap to 50 metres at eight miles, he again extended his advantage and surged along the coast road to the finish in South Shields with Thys 150 metres behind.

Blackheath's Mark Steinle finished third in 1:02.23 with Swindon's Matthew O'Dowd fourth, ahead of Australia's Lee Troop.

The three favourites – World Champion Martin Fiz of Spain, Portugal's Antonia Pinto and the defending champion Thugwane – were disappointing in 6th, 14th and 17th respectively.

Mutai, a Coventry resident since 1994, said: "I planned to go out fast from the start. I knew the course from last year and I was able to hold on to my lead."

Chepchumba, meanwhile, held off a powerful challenge from her Kenyan partner Tegla Loroupe, while someone who would become rather famous in the race was making her half-marathon debut and finishing third. Her name was Paula Radcliffe.

The trio were joined by defending champion Sonia O'Sullivan from Ireland, Portugal's Manuela Machado, Alison Wyeth and another Kenyan Ester Kiplagat in a breakaway group, just after the start.

Radcliffe dropped back to third before closing up to Loroupe again – but the pair were clearly struggling to chase the rapidly disappearing Chepchumba.

The British star Radcliffe insisted: "The crowds were great, and I've always wanted to do this race.

Men's	1st John Mutai (KEN)	1:00:52
	2nd Gert Thys (RSA)	1:01:21
	3rd Mark Steinle	1:02:23
Women's	1st Joyce Chepchumba (KEN)	1:09:07
	2nd Tegla Loroupe (KEN)	1:09:35
	3rd Paula Radcliffe	1:09:37
Wheelchair Men's	Hadj Lahmar	0:49:57
Wheelchair Women's	Tanni Grey Thompson	1:02:32

John Mutai

Joyce Chepchumba

22 October 2000

WHAT a difference a year makes. Paula Radcliffe returned to produce one of the best half-marathon performances the world has seen as the Great North Run marked its 20th birthday.

Radcliffe won in a European half-marathon record of 1:07:07, producing one of the most clinical victories by striking four seconds off Liz McColgan's Euro mark set eight years earlier in Tokyo.

The performance also eclipsed the course record of 1:08:49 set by the legendary figure of Norway's Grete Waitz in 1988.

Radcliffe played down the fact she intended stepping up to the marathon and revealed track racing and the world cross country championship would remain her priorities. She said: "Because you can run fast at this distance doesn't automatically mean you will run a fast marathon."

World marathon champion Tegla Loroupe, the 1993 Great North Run winner, fell off the pace at the five-mile marker and eventually finished exactly three minutes adrift of Radcliffe.

Jelena Prokopcuka, in third place, set a Latvian record of 1:13:56. Radcliffe, third in the previous year's race, was surprised Loroupe's challenge had collapsed so quickly.

"It wasn't so much a case of me putting on the pressure than Tegla starting to struggle. When I sensed she was dropping away, I did increase the pace," said the 26 year old Bedford star.

A men's field bursting at the seams with quality again failed to produce the first ever sub-one hour half-marathon run in Britain.

An astonishing opening mile of 4mins 18 secs from Faustin Baha saw the 18 year old Tanzanian take the lead and never relinquish it. But after such a fast start and the strain of running alone for another dozen miles, Baha slowed considerably in the latter stages before crossing the line in 1:01:51.

The 1999 Kenyan winner, Mutai, could never have forecast that the unknown Londoner Andrew Coleman would catch him with less than three quarters of a mile remaining.

Competing in his first half-marathon, the Enfield runner produced an awesome finish to beat Mutai by six seconds in a time of 1:02:28. "The opportunity was there to make my name and I took it. I ran like a machine and took my chance," said Coleman, 26.

Men's	1st Faustin Baha (TAN)	1:01:51
	2nd Andy Coleman	1:02:28
	3rd John Mutai (KEN)	1:02:34
Women's	1st Paula Radcliffe	1:07:07
	2nd Tegla Loroupe (KEN)	1:10:07
	3rd Jelena Prokopcuka (LAT)	1:13:56
Wheelchair Men's	Kevin Papworth	0:49:18
Wheelchair Women's	Sarah Piercey	1:13:32

1999

On May 6th, elections were held to select representatives for the new devolved governments in Northern Ireland, Scotland and Wales. The low turnout called into question voters' devotion to devolution. Abroad, Britain found herself enmeshed in the Balkans strife for the second time in a decade, when ethnic unrest in the Serbian province of Kosovo erupted into open war. European and American forces were mobilised under the NATO pact. Back in Britain, the nation was shocked by the senseless shooting of TV presenter Jill Dando and the appalling Paddington train crash which claimed the lives of 31 commuters. On a happier note, Prince Edward wed Sophie Rhys-Jones, Victoria Adams, the former 'Posh Spice', married Manchester United star David Beckham and preparations for the Millennium celebrations gathered momentum. The London Eye ferris wheel was hoisted into place opposite Big Ben and the visitor attractions for the Millennium Dome were finally unveiled to the public.

2000

Billions of people celebrated the new decade, century and millennium with some of the most spectacular firework displays ever seen and despite threats of terrorist outrages, the world-wide celebrations passed peaceably. Even the Millennium Bug, the predicted computer chaos supposedly caused by microchips being confused by the new dates, largely failed to materialise. Many projects commissioned to mark the millennium were an outstanding success but some flagship schemes were dogged by problems. The month of May marked a change in fortunes for London politician Ken Livingstone who, despite being expelled from the Labour Party, became the capital's first elected mayor. Apart from the embarrassment of Livingstone's victory, the Labour government faced the most serious challenge to its authority to date when a loose confederation of hauliers, farmers and ordinary motorists demonstrated against the high taxes on UK fuel.

2001

An eerie silence descended on the British countryside when an outbreak of foot and mouth disease led to the slaughter of four million cattle and sheep. Yet such rural devastation paled into insignificance compared with events in New York. On the morning of September 11th, terrorists hijacked four US passenger planes to use as flying bombs. American Airlines flight 11 was crashed into the northern tower of New York's World Trade Centre at 8.48 a.m. Minutes later, United Airlines flight 175 hit the southern tower. Shortly afterwards, the third captured plane, American airlines flight 77, was crashed into the Pentagon but passengers on the fourth airliner overpowered the hijackers. Though their bravery thwarted another attack, the plane crashed into a field killing all on board. An hour later the Trade Centre's twin towers collapsed and the numbers nine/eleven took on a new and sinister meaning. George W Bush declared a 'War on Terror' and launched an invasion of Afghanistan. The Americans claimed that the country's Taliban regime had sheltered the shadowy group of Islamic extremists who called themselves al-Qaeda (meaning 'The Base'), and who had trained the 9:11 terrorists

16 October 2001

DOUBLE world half-marathon champion Paul Tergat was a runaway winner, easily pulling ahead of a world-class field at the halfway point.

But like many before him, the brilliant Kenyan failed in his bid to become the first man to run the distance in under an hour, falling 31 seconds short of his target.

"I believed it was possible to do – but running on your own is hard," said Tergat, feeling the effects of his lonesome performance.

Tergat disposed of the threat posed by fellow-countryman Julius Kimtai who, on his debut over the distance, finished second in 1:01:36 with 1999 champion John Mutai making it a clean sweep of the medals for Kenya.

Britain's Paul Evans, now a 40 year old veteran, finished fifth in a time of 1:03:15 and insisted: "I'm enjoying myself now I'm at this stage of my career. I'm chuffed that I managed to mix it with some of the world's best runners – I finished ahead of some big names."

The women's race went to the wire before world record holder Susan Chepkemei edged ahead of Joyce Chepchumba, the 1999 winner, with less than 500 metres remaining, to record the second fastest Great North Run time ever of 1:08:40.

Pre-race favourite Derartu Tulu, the two-time Olympic 10,000m gold medallist from Ethiopia, finished third as the pair of Kenyans controlled the race. Chepkemei, 26, said: "I was hoping to beat Paula Radcliffe's time but the early pace wasn't fast enough."

First Briton home was Radcliffe's Bedford and County team-mate, 33-year-old Sharon Morris, 14th in a time of 1:14:04.

Men's	1st Paul Tergat (KEN)		1:00:30
	2nd Julius Kimtai (KEN)		1:01:36
	3rd John Mutai (KEN)		1:02:49
Women's	1st Susan Chepkemei (KEN)		1:08:40
	2nd Joyce Chepchumba (KEN)		1:08:45
	3rd Derartu Tulu (ETH)		1:10:13
Wheelchair Men's	Tushar Patel		0:48:10
Wheelchair Women's	Gunilla Wallengren (SWE)		0:52:59

2002

In February 1952 King George the VI had died in his sleep and his daughter had ascended the throne. Fifty years later, Elizabeth the Queen Mother also passed away peacefully age 101. It was predicted that the death of the country's favourite grandmother would mean the celebration of the Queen's Golden Jubilee would be a muted affair, but the nation realised the 'Queen Mum' would have been appalled at such a thought. Official celebrations of the Queen's half century reign began on the 1st of June with a concert of classical music held in the grounds of Buckingham palace, followed three days later by a rock concert. Meanwhile on the continent, the lira, franc, mark and peseta passed into history as twelve European countries adopted the euro as their single common currency.

Paul Tergat

Susan Chepkemei

KENYAN Paul Kosgei, the reigning world half-marathon champion, became the first athlete ever to run the distance in under one hour on British soil.

He entered the record books by overcoming the challenge of Tanzania's John Yuda by four seconds, winning with a telling sprint finish in a time of 59:58. Rodgers Rop, of Kenya, was third in 1:01:40.

That sliced the same margin from the previous UK All-Comers' record by Benson Masya in 1994.

"I knew I was capable of making the record," said Kosgei. "Having Yuda pressure me throughout the race helped me a lot."

Sonia O'Sullivan's second title saw the Irish star run the World's quickest half-marathon time of the year with 1:07:19. The 1998 champion, who hit the front after three miles, scorched along the roads to produce a fine run. Her performance was an Irish record and easily bettered the world leading mark for the year of 1:08:23, achieved by Mizuki Nogchi of Japan in January.

O'Sullivan who a few weeks earlier set a World 10 miles record in the BUPA Great South Run, said: "I came here aiming to run a fast time and obviously I'm delighted with improving on my previous best of 70 mins 5secs. I have to say the last mile really hurt me. I was absolutely shattered and I never thought I would be so glad to see the finishing line."

Behind O'Sullivan there was a spirited performance from Susie Power, the Australian who had been training with the winner during her stay in England and was making her half-marathon debut.

Power was delighted to clock 1:07:56. 1999 champion Joyce Chepchumba was third, the Kenyan crossing the line in 1:08:34.

Men's	1st Paul Kosgei (KEN)	0:59:58
	2nd John Yuda (TAN)	1:00:02
	3rd Rodgers Rop (KEN)	1:01:40
Women's	1st Sonia O'Sullivan (IRL)	1:07:19
	2nd Susie Power (AUS)	1:07:56
	3rd Joyce Chepchumba (KEN)	1:08:34
Wheelchair Men's	Tushar Patel	0:48:46
Wheelchair Women's	Gunilla Wallengren (SWE)	0:57:47

2003

British troops found themselves back in the Persian Gulf supporting an American-led invasion of Iraq. The invasion was the culmination of years of tension in which attempts by the United Nations to discover if Iraq had nuclear and chemical weapons had been continually frustrated. Though the UN failed to unequivocally endorse American calls for military action to resolve the dispute, President Bush assembled an international coalition of forces to promote 'regime change' in Baghdad. There was a brief respite, thanks to the Rugby World Cup. In the Final against the host nation, Jonny Wilkinson sent a last-minute drop kick flying through Australia's goal posts to win the Webb Ellis trophy for England.

Paul Kosgei

Tushar Patel

BRITAIN'S Paula Radcliffe produced a monumental performance, scorching to the fastest half-marathon time the world has ever witnessed – and then insisted her clocking had come as a big surprise.

The course record-holder crossed the line in 1:05:40, slicing four seconds from Susan Chepkemei's previous best, set in Lisbon two years earlier.

Radcliffe ran riot over the 13.1 mile long course from Newcastle to South Shields but said: "It just happened. I knew I was on schedule to break the course record and picked up in the last half mile because I saw the clock on the timekeeping car. But it was only with 30 metres left I realised the world best was possible and I gave it everything I had.

The crowd were magnificent right through the race and particularly in that last mile. But the most important thing was just to win the race. The training sessions beforehand had all gone really well. I was looking forward to it and it was such a great feeling to win the race again."

Three blistering sub-five-minute miles in the second half of the race saw Radcliffe shatter the existing world-best performance at 15 kilometres (46:41).

Then, at 10 miles, Radcliffe was an unbelievable 53 seconds faster than the world record mark set by Kenya's Lornah Kiplagat exactly 12 months ago in Holland.

The aggression of Radcliffe's running continued over the final part of the race, where only a climb between the 10 and 11 mile sector saw her slow to over five-minute-miling.

In the men's race, Hendrik Ramaala also narrowly missed entering the record books. Winner in 1997, the South African clocked the second-fastest time ever on domestic soil, winning by four seconds from Kenya's Jackson Koech in 1:00:01.

Only last year's winner Paul Kosgei – fourth on this occasion – has gone faster in a British race when setting the only sub-60-minute time of 59:58 the previous September.

On target to better the Kenyan's mark, Ramaala said: "I eased off at the end because I was tired. After all, I was a late entry."

Men's	1st Hendrik Ramaala (RSA)	1:00:01
	2nd Jackson Koech (KEN)	1:00:05
	3rd Sergey Lebid (UKR)	1:01:49
Women's	1st Paula Radcliffe	1:05:40
	2nd Berhane Adere (ETH)	1:07:32
	3rd Susan Chepkemei (KEN)	1:07:51
Wheelchair Men's	David Weir	0:45:41
Wheelchair Women's	Gunilla Wallengren (SWE)	0:53:04

Kenny Herriot

Getty Images

Gunilla Wallengren

Mark Shearman

26 September 2004

ETHIOPIAN Dejene Berhanu produced a performance which arguably has only been matched in terms of quality by Paula Radcliffe's victory in 2003.

It was another historic moment for the race because it was the first time an Ethiopian had won it.

Berhanu, who decided to compete in the race only six days after taking part in the 5000m at the IAAF World Athletics final, ran a sensational time of 59:37.

The 23-year-old's time knocked more than 20 seconds off the mark set by Paul Kosgei two years earlier and was all the more impressive coming at the end of an arduous track season.

Berhanu was in contention from the start and was part of a group, including Simon Tonui, the reigning champion Hendrik Ramaala, and Britain's Jon Brown, which made an early breakaway.

The Athens Olympic Games 5,000m fifth-placer, then established a 10 metre lead after four miles which he continued to extend throughout the race.

Berhanu, unaware that he was the first Ethiopian to clinch either the men's or women's title, said: "I am very happy to have done that."

Britain's Jon Brown, who was fourth in the Olympic marathon in Athens a few weeks earlier, revealed he was in the same position when he had a `pitstop' after 10 miles, during which two runners went past him which cost him a higher finish.

He said: "It went as well as I could have hoped for. I realised after three or four miles my legs would not do any more. There are so many good guys out there. I consider myself a similar runner to all three in front of me. I will now take it easy for a couple of weeks and prepare for the next target."

Benita Johnson bounced back from a disappointing Olympic Games 10,000m performance to become the first Australian winner since Lisa Martin completed her hat-trick in 1989.

The 25-year-old World Cross-Country champion, fully recovered from the tendonitis injury which ruined her Athens ambitions, won in a time of 1:07:55.

Only Edith Masai, the world cross-country short course champion and Chepkemei responded, but neither African athlete was in shape to do it again when Johnson made her break for home after 12 miles.

Masai won the race for the line ahead of her Kenyan colleague by five seconds in a time of 1:08.27.

Men's	**1st** Dejene Berhanu (ETH)	0:59:37
	2nd Hendrik Ramaala (RSA)	1:01:38
	3rd Ismaïl Sghyr (FRA)	1:01:39
Women's	**1st** Benita Johnson (AUS)	1:07:55
	2nd Edith Masai (KEN)	1:08:27
	3rd Susan Chepkemei (KEN)	1:08:32
Wheelchair Men's	Kenny Herriot	0:45:37
Wheelchair Women's	Gunilla Wallengren (SWE)	0:52:14

Dejene Berhanu

Mark Shearman

Benita Johnson

Mark Shearman

PAULA RADCLIFFE

my part in it...

World record long distance runner. Best-ever time for the Women's Marathon and twice-winner of the Great North Run.

The first GNR I took part in was in '99. I wanted to take part because I had run the 10k that summer in the World Championships and things had gone well that season and so I made the decision. I'd always watched it on TV and thought the atmosphere looked great and that it looked well organised and I wanted to be part of it. But when it came down to race day, it was the end of season and I was really tired and came third. I was determined to come back and run better the following year.

So in 2000, coming off a disappointing Sydney, I was running well. My form was improving after injury and I felt strong. I remember it being really cold, but it was a sunny day and the crowd were not bothered about how freezing it was, they were just having a good time and there were people out everywhere.

2003 – I was coming back from an annoying shin injury and was looking forward to getting back to racing after a frustrating period. I had done a couple of road races – in Richmond (Nike 10k) and the Flora Light (5k), but I surprised myself with how fast I ran! I broke the European and World records and although they are unofficial records, I actually think it is a tough course because there are more uphills than downhills.

I love running in the North East as the people are very knowledgeable and passionate about athletics and road running.

my part in it...

RUNNING the Great North Run, whatever your time, is a momentous achievement.
This is your opportunity to record some of your own memories of the day(s).

....
....
....
....
....
....
....
....
....
....
....
....
....
....
....
....
....
....
....
....
....
....
....

my part in it...

....
....
....
....
....
....
....
....
....
....
....
....
....
....
....
....
....
....
....

my part in it...

Position & Time

1980.	1996. . . . .
1981.	1997. . . . .
1982.	1998. . . . .
1983.	1999. . . . .
1984.	2000. . . . .
1985.	2001. . . . .
1986.	2002. . . . .
1987.	2003. . . . .
1988.	2004. . . . .
1989.	2005. . . . .
1990.	2006. . . . .
1991.	2007. . . . .
1992.	2008. . . . .
1993.	2009. . . . .
1994.	2010. . . . .
1995.	

THE GREAT NORTH RUN
THE FIRST 25 YEARS
and my part in it